SPIRIT WORLD TRUTHS

From God's Word

Scripture Topics Compiled By

SALLIE DAWKINS

Published by
Firebrand United, LLC
P.O. Box 2506
Danville, Kentucky
40423-2506 USA
www.FirebrandUnited.com

Contents

How to Use This Resource

The spirit realm is real, yet many Christians choose to avoid that part of Jesus' commission which tells us, "These signs will accompany those who believe: in my name they will cast out demons (Mark 16:17)."

I wrestled with this myself. *Why would Jesus instruct us to cast out demons if we're not meant to? Why does this verse say casting out demons is a sign of "those who believe" in Him? Why did Jesus say those who believe in Him will do greater works than He did (John 14:12)? Had this part of the Bible expired? Why wasn't I seeing this happen in any of the churches I attended?*

We have an enemy vying for our attention. Jesus tells us in John 10:10, "the thief only comes to steal, kill, and destroy." Our health, wealth, and well-being are at stake. Satan would love nothing more than to ruin our resources, relationships, ministries, and destiny by tempting us to live in doubt, unbelief, self-destruction, unforgiveness, and accusation of others. Yet Jesus also says, "I came that they may have life, and may have it abundantly (John 10:10)."

Like many Christians, I was unprepared and ill-equipped to fight this invisible battle. The reality of spiritual warfare manifested in my life long before I ever heard anyone speak of such things. I share my testimony of discovering identity, potential, and purpose in Christ within **The Awakening Christian Series**. Learning to align my thoughts, words, and actions with God's Word brought healing and restoration to my life, and I believe it will do the same for you.

Jesus has already won the victory, but it's our job to appropriate or apply this victory in our own lives. The obstacles we overcome here on earth strengthen us for ruling and reigning eternally as kings and priests in the Kingdom of God (Revelation 5:9-10).

Spirit World Truths From God's Word began as a simple word study. God put it on my heart to search for scriptures with "Spirit" or "spirit." You're holding the result in your hands. These scriptures are powerful for helping us to grow in spiritual maturity. God Himself teaches us by His Word and Spirit. As we develop the gift of discerning of spirits (1 Corinthians 12:10), we're able to more effectively intercede in prayer. God hears when our prayers align with His Word. Praying His Word back to Him is a powerful way to break demonic cycles and restore shalom completeness to every aspect of life for all the generations of our bloodline.

God is Spirit. 1 Timothy 1:17, sums it up well, "Now to the King eternal, immortal, invisible, to God who alone is wise, be honor and glory forever and ever. Amen." God created us in His image (Genesis 1:27). Although we have physical bodies, at our core, we are spirit beings (Psalm 139:13). Our spirits will live for eternity, either in heaven or hell, depending on our beliefs. For those who choose not to believe in God, there will be an eternity of darkness and torment in Satan's kingdom (Revelation 20:15). The "good news" of Jesus Christ is that He has paid our sin debt in full and restored us back to our Father (John 3:15, Romans 5:12, Romans 6:22-23).

Within the pages of this book, you'll find over 600 scriptures related to the Spirit of God, man's spirit, demonic spirits, spiritual concepts, and a few helpful verses on spiritual warfare basics. While this is not an exhaustive list of scriptures, it's enough to help get you started on your journey of discovery. World English Bible (WEB) translation was chosen for this project because it's not copyrighted. World English Bible is in the Public Domain and available for everyone to use. I encourage you to study the scriptures here or look them up in your favorite Bible translations. The slight difference in wording between translations is often very eye-opening.

Read each scripture for yourself. Review the context of the text from the surrounding scriptures. Ponder or meditate on how God's Word applies to your life. Trust that God will teach you to wage war and take back all the enemy has stolen (Psalm 144:1). Invite God to grant wisdom for understanding the fullness of the promises of His Word for all your generations.

Yours in Christ,

Sallie Dawkins

PS. In the back of this book, you'll find a list of common spirits and manifestations. A PDF version of these lists is available at www.FirebrandUnited .com.

Spirit of God,
man's spirit, or
demonic spirit?

Spirit of God

Holy Spirit, Spirit of Holiness, Spirit of Jesus Christ, Spirit of Grace, Spirit of Glory

Genesis 1:2 The earth was formless and empty. Darkness was on the surface of the deep and God's Spirit was hovering over the surface of the waters.

Genesis 41:38 Pharaoh said to his servants, "Can we find such a one as this, a man in whom is the Spirit of God?"

Exodus 31:3 I have filled him with the Spirit of God, in wisdom, and in understanding, and in knowledge, and in all kinds of workmanship,

Exodus 35:31 He has filled him with the Spirit of God, in wisdom, in understanding, in knowledge, and in all kinds of workmanship;

Numbers 11:17 I will come down and talk with you there. I will take of the Spirit which is on you, and will put it on them; and they shall bear the burden of the people with you, that you don't bear it yourself alone.

Numbers 11:25 Yahweh came down in the cloud, and spoke to him, and took of the Spirit that was on him, and put it on the seventy elders. When the Spirit rested on them, they prophesied, but they did so no more.

Numbers 11:29 Moses said to him, "Are you jealous for my sake? I wish that all Yahweh's people were prophets, that Yahweh would put his Spirit on them!"

Numbers 11:26 But two men remained in the camp. The name of one was Eldad, and the name of the other Medad; and the Spirit rested on them. They were of those who were written, but had not gone out to the Tent; and they prophesied in the camp.

Numbers 24:2 Balaam lifted up his eyes, and he saw Israel dwelling according to their tribes; and the Spirit of God came on him.

Numbers 27:18 Yahweh said to Moses, "Take Joshua the son of Nun, a man in whom is the Spirit, and lay your hand on him."

Judges 3:10 Yahweh's Spirit came on him, and he judged Israel; and he went out to war, and Yahweh delivered Cushan Rishathaim king of Mesopotamia into his hand. His hand prevailed against Cushan Rishathaim.

Judges 6:34 But Yahweh's Spirit came on Gideon, and he blew a trumpet; and Abiezer was gathered together to follow him.

Judges 11:29 Then Yahweh's Spirit came on Jephthah, and he passed over Gilead and Manasseh, and passed over Mizpah of Gilead, and from Mizpah of Gilead he passed over to the children of Ammon.

Judges 13:25 Yahweh's Spirit began to move him in Mahaneh Dan, between Zorah and Eshtaol.

Judges 14:19 Yahweh's Spirit came mightily on him, and he went down to Ashkelon and struck thirty men of them. He took their plunder, then gave the changes of clothing to those who declared the riddle. His anger burned, and he went up to his father's house.

Judges 15:14 When he came to Lehi, the Philistines shouted as they met him. Then Yahweh's Spirit came mightily on him, and the ropes that were on his arms became as flax that was burned with fire; and his bands dropped from off his hands.

1 Samuel 10:10 When they came there to the hill, behold, a band of prophets met him; and the Spirit of God came mightily on him, and he prophesied among them.

1 Samuel 16:13 Then Samuel took the horn of oil and anointed him in the middle of his brothers. Then Yahweh's Spirit came mightily on David from that day forward. So Samuel rose up and went to Ramah.

1 Samuel 16:14 Now Yahweh's Spirit departed from Saul, and an evil spirit from Yahweh troubled him.

1 Samuel 19:20 Saul sent messengers to seize David: and when they saw the company of the prophets prophesying, and Samuel standing as head over them, God's Spirit came on Saul's messengers, and they also prophesied.

2 Samuel 23:2 "Yahweh's Spirit spoke by me. His word was on my tongue."

1 Kings 22:24 Then Zedekiah the son of Chenaanah came near, and struck Micaiah on the cheek, and said, "Which way did Yahweh's Spirit go from me to speak to you?"

1 Chronicles 12:18 Then the Spirit came on Amasai, who was chief of the thirty, and he said, "We are yours, David, and on your side, you son of Jesse. Peace, peace be to you, and peace be to your helpers; for your God helps you." Then David received them, and made them captains of the band.

1 Chronicles 28:12 ...and the plans of all that he had by the Spirit, for the courts of Yahweh's house, for all the surrounding rooms, for the treasuries of God's house, and for the treasuries of the dedicated things;

2 Chronicles 15:1 The Spirit of God came on Azariah the son of Oded:

2 Chronicles 18:23 Then Zedekiah the son of Chenaanah came near, and struck Micaiah on the cheek, and said, "Which way did Yahweh's Spirit go from me to speak to you?"

2 Chronicles 20:14 Then Yahweh's Spirit came on Jahaziel the son of Zechariah, the son of Benaiah, the son of Jeiel, the son of Mattaniah, the Levite, of the sons of Asaph, in the middle of the assembly;

2 Chronicles 24:20 The Spirit of God came on Zechariah the son of Jehoiada the priest; and he stood above the people, and said to them, "God says, 'Why do you disobey Yahweh's commandments, so that you can't prosper?

Because you have forsaken Yahweh, he has also forsaken you.'"

Nehemiah 9:30 Yet many years you put up with them, and testified against them by your Spirit through your prophets. Yet they would not listen. Therefore you gave them into the hand of the peoples of the lands.

Job 32:8 But there is a spirit in man, and the Spirit of the Almighty gives them understanding.

Job 33:4 The Spirit of God has made me, and the breath of the Almighty gives me life.

Psalm 51:11-12 Don't throw me from your presence, and don't take your Holy Spirit from me. Restore to me the joy of your salvation. Uphold me with a willing spirit.

Psalm 104:30 You send out your Spirit and they are created. You renew the face of the ground.

Psalm 139:7 Where could I go from your Spirit? Or where could I flee from your presence?

Psalm 143:10 Teach me to do your will, for you are my God. Your Spirit is good. Lead me in the land of uprightness.

Isaiah 11:2 Yahweh's Spirit will rest on him: the spirit of wisdom and understanding, the spirit of counsel and might, the spirit of knowledge and of the fear of Yahweh.

Isaiah 34:16 Search in the book of Yahweh, and read: not one of these will be missing. None will lack her mate. For my mouth has commanded, and his Spirit has gathered them.

Isaiah 44:3 For I will pour water on him who is thirsty, and streams on the dry ground. I will pour my Spirit on your descendants, and my blessing on your offspring:

Isaiah 59:21 "As for me, this is my covenant with them," says Yahweh. "My Spirit who is on you, and my words which I have put in your mouth shall not depart out of your mouth, nor out of the mouth of your offspring, nor out of the mouth of your offspring's offspring," says Yahweh, "from now on and forever."

Isaiah 63:11 Then he remembered the days of old, Moses and his people, saying, "Where is he who brought them up out of the sea with the shepherds of his flock? Where is he who put his Holy Spirit among them?"

Ezekiel 3:12 Then the Spirit lifted me up, and I heard behind me the voice of a great rushing, saying, "Blessed be Yahweh's glory from his place."

Ezekiel 3:14 So the Spirit lifted me up, and took me away; and I went in bitterness, in the heat of my spirit; and Yahweh's hand was strong on me.

Ezekiel 8:3 He stretched out the form of a hand, and took me by a lock of my head; and the Spirit lifted me up between earth and the sky, and brought me in the visions of God to Jerusalem, to the door of the gate of the inner court that looks toward the north; where there was the seat of the image of jealousy, which provokes to jealousy.

Ezekiel 11:1 Moreover the Spirit lifted me up, and brought me to the east gate of Yahweh's house, which looks eastward. Behold, twenty-five men were at the door of the gate; and I saw among them Jaazaniah the son of Azzur, and Pelatiah the son of Benaiah, princes of the people.

Ezekiel 11:5 Yahweh's Spirit fell on me, and he said to me, "Speak, 'Yahweh says: "Thus you have said, house of Israel; for I know the things that come into your mind.'"

Ezekiel 11:24 The Spirit lifted me up, and brought me in the vision by the Spirit of God into Chaldea, to the captives. So the vision that I had seen went up from me.

Ezekiel 37:1 Yahweh's hand was on me, and he brought me out in Yahweh's Spirit, and set me down in the middle of the valley; and it was full of bones.

Ezekiel 39:29 "I won't hide my face from them any more; for I have poured out my Spirit on the house of Israel," says the Lord Yahweh.

Joel 2:28-29 "It will happen afterward, that I will pour out my Spirit on all flesh; and your sons and your daughters will prophesy. Your old men will dream dreams. Your young men will see visions. And also on the servants and on the handmaids in those days, I will pour out my Spirit."

Micah 2:7 Shall it be said, O house of Jacob: "Is Yahweh's Spirit angry? Are these his doings? Don't my words do good to him who walks blamelessly?"

Micah 3:8 But as for me, I am full of power by Yahweh's Spirit, and of judgment, and of might, to declare to Jacob his disobedience, and to Israel his sin.

Haggai 2:5 This is the word that I covenanted with you when you came out of Egypt, and my Spirit lived among you. 'Don't be afraid.'

Zechariah 4:6 Then he answered and spoke to me, saying, "This is Yahweh's word to Zerubbabel, saying, 'Not by might, nor by power, but by my Spirit,' says Yahweh of Armies."

Zechariah 7:12 Yes, they made their hearts as hard as flint, lest they might hear the law, and the words which Yahweh of Armies had sent by his Spirit by the former prophets. Therefore great wrath came from Yahweh of Armies.

Matthew 1:18 Now the birth of Jesus Christ was like this: After his mother, Mary, was engaged to Joseph, before they came together, she was found pregnant by the Holy Spirit.

Matthew 1:20 But when he thought about these things, behold, an angel of the Lord appeared to him in a dream, saying, "Joseph, son of David, don't be afraid to take to yourself Mary as your wife, for that which is conceived in her is of the Holy Spirit."

Matthew 3:11 "I indeed baptize you in water for repentance, but he who comes after me is mightier than I, whose sandals I am not worthy to carry. He will baptize you in the Holy Spirit."

Matthew 3:16 Jesus, when he was baptized, went up directly from the water: and behold, the heavens were opened to him. He saw the Spirit of God descending as a dove, and coming on him.

Matthew 4:1 Then Jesus was led up by the Spirit into the wilderness to be tempted by the devil.

Matthew 10:20 For it is not you who speak, but the Spirit of your Father who speaks in you.

Matthew 12:18 "Behold, my servant whom I have chosen, my beloved in whom my soul is well pleased. I will put my Spirit on him. He will proclaim justice to the nations."

Matthew 12:28 But if I by the Spirit of God cast out demons, then God's Kingdom has come upon you.

Matthew 12:31 Therefore I tell you, every sin and blasphemy will be forgiven men, but the blasphemy against the Spirit will not be forgiven men.

Matthew 12:32 Whoever speaks a word against the Son of Man, it will be forgiven him; but whoever speaks against the Holy Spirit, it will not be forgiven him, either in this age, or in that which is to come.

Matthew 28:19 Go and make disciples of all nations, baptizing them in the name of the Father and of the Son and of the Holy Spirit,

Mark 1:8 "I baptized you in water, but he will baptize you in the Holy Spirit."

Mark 1:10 Immediately coming up from the water, he saw the heavens parting and the Spirit descending on him like a dove.

Mark 1:12 Immediately the Spirit drove him out into the wilderness.

Mark 3:28-29 "Most certainly I tell you, all sins of the descendants of man will be forgiven, including their blasphemies with which they may blaspheme; but whoever may blaspheme against the Holy Spirit never has forgiveness, but is subject to eternal condemnation."

Mark 12:36 For David himself said in the Holy Spirit, 'The Lord said to my Lord, "Sit at my right hand, until I make your enemies the footstool of your feet."'

Mark 13:11 When they lead you away and deliver you up, don't be anxious beforehand, or premeditate what you will say, but say whatever will be given you in that hour. For it is not you who speak, but the Holy Spirit.

Luke 1:15 For he will be great in the sight of the Lord, and he will drink no wine nor strong drink. He will be filled with the Holy Spirit, even from his mother's womb.

Luke 1:35 The angel answered her, "The Holy Spirit will come on you, and the power of the Most High will overshadow you. Therefore also the holy one who is born from you will be called the Son of God."

Luke 1:41 When Elizabeth heard Mary's greeting, the baby leaped in her womb; and Elizabeth was filled with the Holy Spirit.

Luke 1:67-68 His father Zacharias was filled with the Holy Spirit, and prophesied, saying, "Blessed be the Lord, the God of Israel, for he has visited and redeemed his people;"

Luke 2:25 Behold, there was a man in Jerusalem whose name was Simeon. This man was righteous and devout, looking for the consolation of Israel, and the Holy Spirit was on him.

Luke 2:26 It had been revealed to him by the Holy Spirit that he should not see death before he had seen the Lord's Christ

Luke 2:27 He came in the Spirit into the temple. When the parents brought in the child, Jesus, that they might do concerning him according to the custom of the law,

Luke 3:16 John answered them all, "I indeed baptize you with water, but he comes who is mightier than I, the strap of whose sandals I am not worthy to loosen. He will baptize you in the Holy Spirit and fire,"

Luke 3:22 ...and the Holy Spirit descended in a bodily form like a dove on him; and a voice came out of the sky, saying "You are my beloved Son. In you I am well pleased."

Luke 4:1 Jesus, full of the Holy Spirit, returned from the Jordan, and was led by the Spirit into the wilderness

Luke 4:14 Jesus returned in the power of the Spirit into Galilee, and news about him spread through all the surrounding area.

Luke 4:18 "The Spirit of the Lord is on me, because he has anointed me to preach good news to the poor. He has sent me to heal the broken hearted, to proclaim release to the captives, recovering of sight to the blind, to deliver those who are crushed,"

Luke 10:21 In that same hour Jesus rejoiced in the Holy Spirit, and said, "I thank you, O Father, Lord of heaven and earth, that you have hidden these things from the wise and understanding, and revealed them to little children. Yes, Father, for so it was well-pleasing in your sight."

Luke 11:13 "If you then, being evil, know how to give good gifts to your children, how much more will your heavenly Father give the Holy Spirit to those who ask him?"

Luke 12:10 Everyone who speaks a word against the Son of Man will be forgiven, but those who blaspheme against the Holy Spirit will not be forgiven.

Luke 12:12 "...for the Holy Spirit will teach you in that same hour what you must say."

John 1:32 John testified, saying, "I have seen the Spirit descending like a dove out of heaven, and it remained on him."

John 1:33 I didn't recognize him, but he who sent me to baptize in water said to me, 'On whomever you will see the Spirit descending and remaining on him is he who baptizes in the Holy Spirit.'

John 3:6 That which is born of the flesh is flesh. That which is born of the Spirit is spirit.

John 3:8 "The wind blows where it wants to, and you hear its sound, but don't know where it comes from and where it is going. So is everyone who is born of the Spirit."

John 3:34 For he whom God has sent speaks the words of God; for God gives the Spirit without measure.

John 7:39 But he said this about the Spirit, which those believing in him were to receive. For the Holy Spirit was not yet given, because Jesus wasn't yet glorified.

John 14:17 ...the Spirit of truth, whom the world can't receive; for it doesn't see him and doesn't know him. You know him, for he lives with you, and will be in you.

John 14:26 But the Counselor, the Holy Spirit, whom the Father will send in my name, will teach you all things, and will remind you of all that I said to you.

John 15:26 "When the Counselor has come, whom I will send to you from the Father, the Spirit of truth, who proceeds from the Father, he will testify about me."

John 16:13 However when he, the Spirit of truth, has come, he will guide you into all truth, for he will not speak from himself; but whatever he hears, he will speak. He will declare to you things that are coming.

John 20:22 When he had said this, he breathed on them, and said to them, "Receive the Holy Spirit!"

Acts 1:2 ...until the day in which he was received up, after he had given commandment through the Holy Spirit to the apostles whom he had chosen.

Acts 1:5 "For John indeed baptized in water, but you will be baptized in the Holy Spirit not many days from now."

Acts 1:8 "But you will receive power when the Holy Spirit has come upon you. You will be witnesses to me in Jerusalem, in all Judea and Samaria, and to the uttermost parts of the earth."

Acts 1:16 "Brothers, it was necessary that this Scripture should be fulfilled, which the Holy Spirit spoke before by the mouth of David concerning Judas, who was guide to those who took Jesus."

Acts 2:4 They were all filled with the Holy Spirit, and began to speak with other languages, as the Spirit gave them the ability to speak.

Acts 2:33 Being therefore exalted by the right hand of God, and having received from the Father the promise of the Holy Spirit, he has poured out this, which you now see and hear.

Acts 2:38 Peter said to them, "Repent, and be baptized, every one of you, in the name of Jesus Christ for the forgiveness of sins, and you will receive the gift of the Holy Spirit."

Acts 4:8 Then Peter, filled with the Holy Spirit, said to them, "You rulers of the people, and elders of Israel,"

Acts 4:31 When they had prayed, the place was shaken where they were gathered together. They were all filled with the Holy Spirit, and they spoke the word of God with boldness.

Acts 5:3 But Peter said, "Ananias, why has Satan filled your heart to lie to the Holy Spirit and to keep back part of the price of the land?"

Acts 5:9 But Peter asked her, "How is it that you have agreed together to tempt the Spirit of the Lord? Behold, the feet of those who have buried your husband are at the door, and they will carry you out."

Acts 5:32 "We are his witnesses of these things; and so also is the Holy Spirit, whom God has given to those who obey him."

Acts 6:3 Therefore select from among you, brothers, seven men of good report, full of the Holy Spirit and of wisdom, whom we may appoint over this business.

Acts 6:5 These words pleased the whole multitude. They chose Stephen, a man full of faith and of the Holy Spirit, Philip, Prochorus, Nicanor, Timon, Parmenas, and Nicolaus, a proselyte of Antioch;

Acts 7:51 "You stiff-necked and uncircumcised in heart and ears, you always resist the Holy Spirit! As your fathers did, so you do."

Acts 7:55 But he, being full of the Holy Spirit, looked up steadfastly into heaven and saw the glory of God, and Jesus standing on the right hand of God,

Acts 8:14-15 Now when the apostles who were at Jerusalem heard that Samaria had received the word of God, they sent Peter and John to them, who, when they had come down, prayed for them, that they might receive the Holy Spirit;

Acts 8:18-19 Now when Simon saw that the Holy Spirit was given through the laying on of the apostles' hands, he offered them money, saying, "Give me also this power, that whomever I lay my hands on may receive the Holy Spirit."

Acts 8:39 When they came up out of the water, the Spirit of the Lord caught Philip away, and the eunuch didn't see him any more, for he went on his way rejoicing.

Acts 9:17 Ananias departed and entered into the house. Laying his hands on him, he said, "Brother Saul, the Lord, who appeared to you on the road by which you came, has sent me that you may receive your sight and be filled with the Holy Spirit."

Acts 9:31 So the assemblies throughout all Judea, Galilee, and Samaria had peace, and were built up. They were multiplied, walking in the fear of the Lord and in the comfort of the Holy Spirit.

Acts 10:38 ...even Jesus of Nazareth, how God anointed him with the Holy Spirit and with power, who went about doing good and healing all who were oppressed by the devil, for God was with him.

Acts 10:44 While Peter was still speaking these words, the Holy Spirit fell on all those who heard the word.

Acts 10:45 They of the circumcision who believed were amazed, as many as came with Peter, because the gift of the Holy Spirit was also poured out on the Gentiles.

Acts 10:47 "Can anyone forbid these people from being baptized with water? They have received the Holy Spirit just like us."

Acts 11:15 As I began to speak, the Holy Spirit fell on them, even as on us at the beginning.

Acts 11:16 I remembered the word of the Lord, how he said, 'John indeed baptized in water, but you will be baptized in the Holy Spirit.'

Acts 11:24 For he was a good man, and full of the Holy Spirit and of faith, and many people were added to the Lord.

Acts 11:28 One of them named Agabus stood up, and indicated by the Spirit that there should be a great famine all over the world, which also happened in the days of Claudius.

Acts 13:2 As they served the Lord and fasted, the Holy Spirit said, "Separate Barnabas and Saul for me, for the work to which I have called them."

Acts 13:4 So, being sent out by the Holy Spirit, they went down to Seleucia. From there they sailed to Cyprus.

Acts 13:9–10 But Saul, who is also called Paul, filled with the Holy Spirit, fastened his eyes on him, and said, "You son of the devil, full of all deceit and all cunning, you enemy of all righteousness, will you not cease to pervert the right ways of the Lord?"

Acts 13:52 The disciples were filled with joy and with the Holy Spirit.

Acts 15:8 God, who knows the heart, testified about them, giving them the Holy Spirit, just like he did to us.

Acts 15:28 For it seemed good to the Holy Spirit, and to us, to lay no greater burden on you than these necessary things:

Acts 16:6 When they had gone through the region of Phrygia and Galatia, they were forbidden by the Holy Spirit to speak the word in Asia.

Acts 19:2 He said to them, "Did you receive the Holy Spirit when you believed?" They said to him, "No, we haven't even heard that there is a Holy Spirit."

Acts 19:6 When Paul had laid his hands on them, the Holy Spirit came on them and they spoke with other languages and prophesied.

Acts 20:2–23 Now, behold, I go bound by the Spirit to Jerusalem, not knowing what will happen to me there; except that the Holy Spirit testifies in every city, saying that bonds and afflictions wait for me.

Acts 20:28 Take heed, therefore, to yourselves, and to all the flock, in which the Holy Spirit has made you overseers, to shepherd the assembly of the Lord and God which he purchased with his own blood.

Acts 21:4 Having found disciples, we stayed there seven days. These said to Paul through the Spirit that he should not go up to Jerusalem.

Acts 21:11 Coming to us and taking Paul's belt, he bound his own feet and hands, and said, "The Holy Spirit says: 'So the Jews at Jerusalem will bind the man who owns this belt, and will deliver him into the hands of the Gentiles.'"

Acts 28:25 When they didn't agree among themselves, they departed after Paul had spoken one word, "The Holy Spirit spoke rightly through Isaiah the prophet to our fathers,"

Romans 1:4 ...who was declared to be the Son of God with power, according to the Spirit of holiness, by the resurrection from the dead, Jesus Christ our Lord,

Romans 5:5 ...and hope doesn't disappoint us, because God's love has been poured into our hearts through the Holy Spirit who was given to us.

Romans 8:1 There is therefore now no condemnation to those who are in Christ Jesus, who don't walk according to the flesh, but according to the Spirit.

Romans 8:2 For the law of the Spirit of life in Christ Jesus made me free from the law of sin and of death.

Romans 8:4 ...that the ordinance of the law might be fulfilled in us, who walk not after the flesh, but after the Spirit.

Romans 8:5 For those who live according to the flesh set their minds on the things of the flesh, but those who live according to the Spirit, the things of the Spirit.

Romans 8:6 For the mind of the flesh is death, but the mind of the Spirit is life and peace;

Romans 8:9 But you are not in the flesh but in the Spirit, if it is so that the Spirit of God dwells in you. But if any man doesn't have the Spirit of Christ, he is not his.

Romans 8:11 But if the Spirit of him who raised up Jesus from the dead dwells in you, he who raised up Christ Jesus from the dead will also give life to your mortal bodies through his Spirit who dwells in you.

Romans 8:13 For if you live after the flesh, you must die; but if by the Spirit you put to death the deeds of the body, you will live.

Romans 8:14 For as many as are led by the Spirit of God, these are children of God.

Romans 8:15 For you didn't receive the spirit of bondage again to fear, but you received the Spirit of adoption, by whom we cry, "Abba! Father!"

Romans 8:16 The Spirit himself testifies with our spirit that we are children of God;

Romans 8:23 Not only so, but ourselves also, who have the first fruits of the Spirit, even we ourselves groan within ourselves, waiting for adoption, the redemption of our body.

Romans 8:26 In the same way, the Spirit also helps our weaknesses, for we don't know how to pray as we ought. But the Spirit himself makes intercession for us with groanings which can't be uttered.

Romans 8:27 He who searches the hearts knows what is on the Spirit's mind, because he makes intercession for the saints according to God.

Romans 9:1–2 I tell the truth in Christ. I am not lying, my conscience testifying with me in the Holy Spirit that I have great sorrow and unceasing pain in my heart.

Romans 14:17 ...for God's Kingdom is not eating and drinking, but righteousness, peace, and joy in the Holy Spirit.

Romans 15:13 Now may the God of hope fill you with all joy and peace in believing, that you may abound in hope, in the power of the Holy Spirit.

Romans 15:16 ...that I should be a servant of Christ Jesus to the Gentiles, serving as a priest of the Good

News of God, that the offering up of the Gentiles might be made acceptable, sanctified by the Holy Spirit.

Romans 15:19 ...in the power of signs and wonders, in the power of God's Spirit; so that from Jerusalem, and around as far as to Illyricum, I have fully preached the Good News of Christ;

Romans 15:30 Now I beg you, brothers, by our Lord Jesus Christ and by the love of the Spirit, that you strive together with me in your prayers to God for me,

1 Corinthians 2:4 My speech and my preaching were not in persuasive words of human wisdom, but in demonstration of the Spirit and of power,

1 Corinthians 2:10 But to us, God revealed them through the Spirit. For the Spirit searches all things, yes, the deep things of God.

1 Corinthians 2:11 For who among men knows the things of a man, except the spirit of the man, which is in him? Even so, no one knows the things of God, except God's Spirit.

1 Corinthians 2:12 But we received not the spirit of the world, but the Spirit which is from God, that we might know the things that were freely given to us by God.

1 Corinthians 2:13 We also speak these things, not in words which man's wisdom teaches, but which the Holy Spirit teaches, comparing spiritual things with spiritual things.

1 Corinthians 2:14 Now the natural man doesn't receive the things of God's Spirit, for they are foolishness to him, and he can't know them, because they are spiritually discerned.

1 Corinthians 3:16 Don't you know that you are a temple of God, and that God's Spirit lives in you?

1 Corinthians 6:11 Some of you were such, but you were washed. But you were sanctified. But you were justified in the name of the Lord Jesus, and in the Spirit of our God.

1 Corinthians 6:19 Or don't you know that your body is a temple of the Holy Spirit who is in you, whom you have from God? You are not your own,

1 Corinthians 12:3 Therefore I make known to you that no man speaking by God's Spirit says, "Jesus is accursed." No one can say, "Jesus is Lord," but by the Holy Spirit.

1 Corinthians 12:4 Now there are various kinds of gifts, but the same Spirit.

1 Corinthians 12:7 But to each one is given the manifestation of the Spirit for the profit of all.

1 Corinthians 12:8 For to one is given through the Spirit the word of wisdom, and to another the word of knowledge, according to the same Spirit;

1 Corinthians 12:9-10 ...to another faith, by the same Spirit; and to another gifts of healings, by the same Spirit; and to another workings of miracles; and to another prophecy; and to another discerning of spirits; to another different kinds of languages; and to another the interpretation of languages.

1 Corinthians 12:11 But the one and the same Spirit produces all of these, distributing to each one separately as he desires.

2 Corinthians 1:22 ...who also sealed us, and gave us the down payment of the Spirit in our hearts.

2 Corinthians 3:3 ...being revealed that you are a letter of Christ, served by us, written not with ink, but with the Spirit of the living God; not in tablets of stone, but in tablets that are hearts of flesh.

2 Corinthians 3:6 ...who also made us sufficient as servants of a new covenant, not of the letter, but of the Spirit. For the letter kills, but the Spirit gives life.

2 Corinthians 3:8 ...won't service of the Spirit be with much more glory?

2 Corinthians 3:17 Now the Lord is the Spirit and where the Spirit of the Lord is, there is liberty.

2 Corinthians 3:18 But we all, with unveiled face seeing the glory of the Lord as in a mirror, are transformed into the same image from glory to glory, even as from the Lord, the Spirit.

2 Corinthians 5:5 Now he who made us for this very thing is God, who also gave to us the down payment of the Spirit.

2 Corinthians 6:6 ...in pureness, in knowledge, in perseverance, in kindness, in the Holy Spirit, in sincere love,

2 Corinthians 13:14 The grace of the Lord Jesus Christ, God's love, and the fellowship of the Holy Spirit be with you all. Amen.

Galatians 3:2 I just want to learn this from you: Did you receive the Spirit by the works of the law, or by hearing of faith?

Galatians 3:3 Are you so foolish? Having begun in the Spirit, are you now completed in the flesh?

Galatians 3:5 He therefore who supplies the Spirit to you and does miracles among you, does he do it by the works of the law, or by hearing of faith?

Galatians 3:14 ...that the blessing of Abraham might come on the Gentiles through Christ Jesus, that we might receive the promise of the Spirit through faith.

Galatians 4:6 And because you are children, God sent out the Spirit of his Son into your hearts, crying, "Abba, Father!"

Galatians 5:5 For we, through the Spirit, by faith wait for the hope of righteousness.

Galatians 5:16 But I say, walk by the Spirit, and you won't fulfill the lust of the flesh.

Galatians 5:17 For the flesh lusts against the Spirit, and the Spirit against the flesh; and these are contrary to one another, that you may not do the things that you desire.

Galatians 5:18 But if you are led by the Spirit, you are not under the law.

Galatians 5:22-23 But the fruit of the Spirit is love, joy, peace, patience, kindness, goodness, faith, gentleness, and self-control. Against such things there is no law.

Galatians 5:25 If we live by the Spirit, let's also walk by the Spirit.

Galatians 6:8 For he who sows to his own flesh will from the flesh reap corruption. But he who sows to the Spirit will from the Spirit reap eternal life.

Ephesians 1:13 In him you also, having heard the word of the truth, the Good News of your salvation—in whom, having also believed, you were sealed with the promised Holy Spirit,

Ephesians 2:18 For through him we both have our access in one Spirit to the Father.

Ephesians 2:22 ...in whom you also are built together for a habitation of God in the Spirit.

Ephesians 3:5 ...which in other generations was not made known to the children of men, as it has now been revealed to his holy apostles and prophets in the Spirit,

Ephesians 3:16 ...that he would grant you, according to the riches of his glory, that you may be strengthened with power through his Spirit in the inner person,

Ephesians 4:3 ...being eager to keep the unity of the Spirit in the bond of peace.

Ephesians 4:4 There is one body and one Spirit, even as you also were called in one hope of your calling,

Ephesians 4:30 Don't grieve the Holy Spirit of God, in whom you were sealed for the day of redemption.

Ephesians 5:9 ...for the fruit of the Spirit is in all goodness and righteousness and truth,

Ephesians 5:18 Don't be drunken with wine, in which is dissipation, but be filled with the Spirit,

Ephesians 6:17 And take the helmet of salvation, and the sword of the Spirit, which is the word of God;

Ephesians 6:18 ...with all prayer and requests, praying at all times in the Spirit, and being watchful to this end in all perseverance and requests for all the saints:

Philippians 1:19 For I know that this will turn out to my salvation, through your prayers and the supply of the Spirit of Jesus Christ,

Philippians 2:1 If therefore there is any exhortation in Christ, if any consolation of love, if any fellowship of the Spirit, if any tender mercies and compassion,

Philippians 3:3 For we are the circumcision, who worship God in the Spirit, and rejoice in Christ Jesus, and have no confidence in the flesh;

Colossians 1:8 ...who also declared to us your love in the Spirit.

1 Thessalonians 1:5 ...and that our Good News came to you not in word only, but also in power, and in the Holy Spirit, and with much assurance. You know what kind of men we showed ourselves to be among you for your sake.

1 Thessalonians 1:6 You became imitators of us and of the Lord, having received the word in much affliction, with joy of the Holy Spirit,

1 Thessalonians 4:8 Therefore he who rejects this doesn't reject man, but God, who has also given his Holy Spirit to you.

1 Thessalonians 5:19 Don't quench the Spirit.

2 Thessalonians 2:13 But we are bound to always give thanks to God for you, brothers loved by the Lord, because God chose you from the beginning for salvation through sanctification of the Spirit and belief in the truth,

1 Timothy 4:1 But the Spirit says expressly that in later times some will fall away from the faith, paying attention to seducing spirits and doctrines of demons,

2 Timothy 1:14 That good thing which was committed to you, guard through the Holy Spirit who dwells in us.

Titus 3:5 ...not by works of righteousness which we did ourselves, but according to his mercy, he saved us through the washing of regeneration and renewing by the Holy Spirit,

Hebrews 2:4 God also testifying with them, both by signs and wonders, by various works of power and by gifts of the Holy Spirit, according to his own will?

Hebrews 6:4 For concerning those who were once enlightened and tasted of the heavenly gift, and were made partakers of the Holy Spirit,

Hebrews 9:8 The Holy Spirit is indicating this, that the way into the Holy Place wasn't yet revealed while the first tabernacle was still standing.

Hebrews 9:14 ...how much more will the blood of Christ, who through the eternal Spirit offered himself without defect to God, cleanse your conscience from dead works to serve the living God?

Hebrews 10:15–16 The Holy Spirit also testifies to us, for after saying, "This is the covenant that I will make with them: 'After those days,' says the Lord, 'I will put my laws on their heart, I will also write them on their mind;"

Hebrews 10:29 How much worse punishment do you think he will be judged worthy of who has trodden under foot the Son of God, and has counted the blood of the covenant with which he was sanctified an unholy thing, and has insulted the Spirit of grace?

1 Peter 1:2 ...according to the foreknowledge of God the Father, in sanctification of the Spirit, that you may obey Jesus Christ and be sprinkled with his blood: Grace to you and peace be multiplied.

1 Peter 1:11 ...searching for who or what kind of time the Spirit of Christ, which was in them, pointed to, when he predicted the sufferings of Christ, and the glories that would follow them.

1 Peter 1:12 To them it was revealed, that they served not themselves, but you, in these things, which now have been announced to you through those who preached the Good News to you by the Holy Spirit sent out from heaven; which things angels desire to look into.

1 Peter 1:22 Seeing you have purified your souls in your obedience to the truth through the Spirit in sincere brotherly affection, love one another from the heart fervently,

1 Peter 3:18 Because Christ also suffered for sins once, the righteous for the unrighteous, that he might bring you to God, being put to death in the flesh, but made alive in the Spirit,

1 Peter 4:14 If you are insulted for the name of Christ, you are blessed; because the Spirit of glory and of God rests on you. On their part he is blasphemed, but on your part he is glorified.

2 Peter 1:21 For no prophecy ever came by the will of man: but holy men of God spoke, being moved by the Holy Spirit.

1 John 3:24 He who keeps his commandments remains in him, and he in him. By this we know that he remains in us, by the Spirit which he gave us.

1 John 4:2 By this you know the Spirit of God: every spirit who confesses that Jesus Christ has come in the flesh is of God,

1 John 4:13 By this we know that we remain in him and he in us, because he has given us of his Spirit.

1 John 5:6 This is he who came by water and blood, Jesus Christ; not with the water only, but with the water and the blood. It is the Spirit who testifies, because the Spirit is the truth.

1 John 5:7-8 For there are three who testify: the Spirit, the water, and the blood; and the three agree as one.

Jude 1:19-20 These are those who cause divisions and are sensual, not having the Spirit. But you, beloved, keep building up yourselves on your most holy faith, praying in the Holy Spirit.

Revelation 2:7 He who has an ear, let him hear what the Spirit says to the assemblies. To him who overcomes I will give to eat from the tree of life, which is in the Paradise of my God.

Revelation 2:11 He who has an ear, let him hear what the Spirit says to the assemblies. He who overcomes won't be harmed by the second death.

Revelation 2:17 He who has an ear, let him hear what the Spirit says to the assemblies. To him who overcomes, to him I will give of the hidden manna, and I will give him a white stone, and on the stone a new name written, which no one knows but he who receives it.

Revelation 2:29 He who has an ear, let him hear what the Spirit says to the assemblies.

Revelation 3:1 And to the angel of the assembly in Sardis write: He who has the seven Spirits of God and the seven stars says these things: I know your works, that you have a reputation of being alive, but you are dead.

Revelation 3:6 He who has an ear, let him hear what the Spirit says to the assemblies.

Revelation 3:13 He who has an ear, let him hear what the Spirit says to the assemblies.

Revelation 3:22 He who has an ear, let him hear what the Spirit says to the assemblies.

Revelation 4:5 Out of the throne proceed lightnings, sounds, and thunders. There were seven lamps of fire burning before his throne, which are the seven Spirits of God.

Revelation 5:6 I saw in the middle of the throne and of the four living creatures, and in the middle of the elders, a Lamb standing, as though it had been slain, having seven horns and seven eyes, which are the seven Spirits of God, sent out into all the earth.

Revelation 14:13 I heard a voice from heaven saying, "Write, 'Blessed are the dead who die in the Lord from now on.'" "Yes," says the Spirit, "that they may rest from their labors; for their works follow with them."

Revelation 17:3 He carried me away in the Spirit into a wilderness. I saw a woman sitting on a scarlet-colored beast, full of blasphemous names, having seven heads and ten horns.

Revelation 19:10 I fell down before his feet to worship him. He said to me, "Look! Don't do it! I am a fellow bondservant with you and with your brothers who hold the testimony of Jesus. Worship God, for the testimony of Jesus is the Spirit of Prophecy."

Revelation 21:10 He carried me away in the Spirit to a great and high mountain, and showed me the holy city, Jerusalem, coming down out of heaven from God,

Revelation 22:17 The Spirit and the bride say, "Come!" He who hears, let him say, "Come!" He who is thirsty, let him come. He who desires, let him take the water of life freely.

Spirit of Man

Man's Spirit, Spirits of All Flesh

Genesis 25:8 Abraham gave up his spirit, and died at a good old age, an old man, and full of years, and was gathered to his people.

Genesis 25:17 These are the years of the life of Ishmael: one hundred thirty-seven years. He gave up his spirit and died, and was gathered to his people.

Genesis 35:29 Isaac gave up the spirit and died, and was gathered to his people, old and full of days. Esau and Jacob, his sons, buried him.

Genesis 41:8 In the morning, his spirit was troubled, and he sent and called for all of Egypt's magicians and wise men. Pharaoh told them his dreams, but there was no one who could interpret them to Pharaoh.

Genesis 45:27 They told him all the words of Joseph, which he had said to them. When he saw the wagons which Joseph had sent to carry him, the spirit of Jacob, their father, revived.

Exodus 35:21 They came, everyone whose heart stirred him up, and everyone whom his spirit made willing, and brought Yahweh's offering for the work of the Tent of Meeting, and for all of its service, and for the holy garments.

Numbers 14:24 But my servant Caleb, because he had another spirit with him, and has followed me fully, him I will bring into the land into which he went. His offspring shall possess it.

Numbers 16:22 They fell on their faces, and said, "God, the God of the spirits of all flesh, shall one man sin, and will you be angry with all the congregation?"

Numbers 27:16 "Let Yahweh, the God of the spirits of all flesh, appoint a man over the congregation,"

Deuteronomy 2:30 But Sihon king of Heshbon would not let us pass by him; for Yahweh your God hardened his spirit and made his heart obstinate, that he might deliver him into your hand, as it is today.

Joshua 2:11 As soon as we had heard it, our hearts melted, and there wasn't any more spirit in any man, because of you: for Yahweh your God, he is God in heaven above, and on earth beneath.

Joshua 5:1 When all the kings of the Amorites, who were beyond the Jordan westward, and all the kings of the Canaanites, who were by the sea, heard how Yahweh had dried up the waters of the Jordan from before the children of Israel until we had crossed over, their heart melted, and there was no more spirit in them, because of the children of Israel.

Judges 15:19 But God split the hollow place that is in Lehi, and water came out of it. When he had drunk, his spirit came again, and he revived. Therefore its name was called En Hakkore, which is in Lehi, to this day.

1 Samuel 1:15 Hannah answered, "No, my lord, I am a woman of a sorrowful spirit. I have not been drinking wine or strong drink, but I poured out my soul before Yahweh."

1 Samuel 30:12 They gave him a piece of a cake of figs, and two clusters of raisins. When he had eaten, his spirit came again to him; for he had eaten no bread, and drank no water for three days and three nights.

1 Chronicles 5:26 So the God of Israel stirred up the spirit of Pul king of Assyria, and the spirit of Tilgath Pilneser king of Assyria, and he carried them away, even the Reubenites, and the Gadites, and the half-tribe of Manasseh, and brought them to Halah, Habor, Hara, and to the river of Gozan, to this day.

2 Chronicles 36:22 Now in the first year of Cyrus king of Persia, that Yahweh's word by the mouth of Jeremiah might be accomplished, Yahweh stirred up the spirit of Cyrus king of Persia, so that he made a proclamation throughout all his kingdom, and put it also in writing, saying,

Ezra 1:1 Now in the first year of Cyrus king of Persia, that Yahweh's word by Jeremiah's mouth might be accomplished, Yahweh stirred up the spirit of Cyrus king of Persia, so that he made a proclamation throughout all his kingdom, and put it also in writing, saying,

Ezra 1:5 Then the heads of fathers' households of Judah and Benjamin, the priests, and the Levites, all whose spirit God had stirred to go up rose up to build Yahweh's house which is in Jerusalem.

Job 6:4 For the arrows of the Almighty are within me. My spirit drinks up their poison. The terrors of God set themselves in array against me.

Job 7:11 "Therefore I will not keep silent. I will speak in the anguish of my spirit. I will complain in the bitterness of my soul."

Job 10:18 "'Why, then, have you brought me out of the womb? I wish I had given up the spirit, and no eye had seen me."

Job 11:20 "But the eyes of the wicked will fail. They will have no way to flee. Their hope will be the giving up of the spirit."

Job 15:13 ...that you turn your spirit against God, and let such words go out of your mouth?

Job 20:3 I have heard the reproof which puts me to shame. The spirit of my understanding answers me.

Job 26:4 To whom have you uttered words? Whose spirit came out of you?

Job 32:18 For I am full of words. The spirit within me constrains me.

Psalm 31:5 Into your hand I commend my spirit. You redeem me, Yahweh, God of truth.

Psalm 32:2 Blessed is the man to whom Yahweh doesn't impute iniquity, in whose spirit there is no deceit.

Psalm 51:11–12 Don't throw me from your presence, and don't take your Holy Spirit from me. Restore to me the joy of your salvation. Uphold me with a willing spirit.

Psalm 77:3 I remember God, and I groan. I complain, and my spirit is overwhelmed. Selah.

Psalm 78:8 ...and might not be as their fathers, a stubborn and rebellious generation, a generation that didn't make their hearts loyal, whose spirit was not steadfast with God.

Psalm 143:3-4 For the enemy pursues my soul. He has struck my life down to the ground. He has made me live in dark places, as those who have been long dead. Therefore my spirit is overwhelmed within me. My heart within me is desolate.

Proverbs 15:4 A gentle tongue is a tree of life, but deceit in it crushes the spirit.

Proverbs 20:27 The spirit of man is Yahweh's lamp, searching all his innermost parts.

Proverbs 21:16 The man who wanders out of the way of understanding shall rest in the assembly of the departed spirits.

Proverbs 29:23 A man's pride brings him low, but one of lowly spirit gains honor.

Ecclesiastes 3:21 "Who knows the spirit of man, whether it goes upward, and the spirit of the animal, whether it goes downward to the earth?"

Ecclesiastes 7:8 Better is the end of a thing than its beginning. The patient in spirit is better than the proud in spirit.

Ecclesiastes 8:8 There is no man who has power over the spirit to contain the spirit; neither does he have power over the day of death. There is no discharge in war; neither shall wickedness deliver those who practice it.

Ecclesiastes 12:7 ...and the dust returns to the earth as it was, and the spirit returns to God who gave it.

Isaiah 26:9 With my soul I have desired you in the night. Yes, with my spirit within me I will seek you earnestly; for when your judgments are in the earth, the inhabitants of the world learn righteousness.

Isaiah 38:16 Lord, men live by these things; and my spirit finds life in all of them: you restore me, and cause me to live.

Isaiah 42:5 God Yahweh, he who created the heavens and stretched them out, he who spread out the earth and that which comes out of it, he who gives breath to its people and spirit to those who walk in it, says:

Jeremiah 51:11 "Make the arrows sharp! Hold the shields firmly! Yahweh has stirred up the spirit of the kings of the Medes, because his purpose is against Babylon, to destroy it; for it is the vengeance of Yahweh, the vengeance of his temple."

Ezekiel 11:19 I will give them one heart, and I will put a new spirit within you. I will take the stony heart out of their flesh, and will give them a heart of flesh;

Ezekiel 13:3 The Lord Yahweh says, "Woe to the foolish prophets, who follow their own spirit, and have seen nothing!"

Ezekiel 18:31 Cast away from you all your transgressions, in which you have transgressed; and make yourself a new heart and a new spirit: for why will you die, house of Israel?

Ezekiel 21:7 "It shall be, when they ask you, 'Why do you sigh?' that you shall say, 'Because of the news, for it comes! Every heart will melt, all hands will be feeble, every spirit will faint, and all knees will be weak as water. Behold, it comes, and it shall be done, says the Lord Yahweh.'"

Ezekiel 36:26 I will also give you a new heart, and I will put a new spirit within you. I will take away the stony heart out of your flesh, and I will give you a heart of flesh.

Daniel 2:1 In the second year of the reign of Nebuchadnezzar, Nebuchadnezzar dreamed dreams; and his spirit was troubled, and his sleep went from him.

Haggai 1:14 Yahweh stirred up the spirit of Zerubbabel, the son of Shealtiel, governor of Judah, and the spirit of Joshua, the son of Jehozadak, the high priest, and the spirit of all the remnant of the people; and they came and worked on the house of Yahweh of Armies, their God,

Zechariah 12:1 A revelation: Yahweh's word concerning Israel. Yahweh, who stretches out the heavens, and lays the foundation of the earth, and forms the spirit of man within him says:

Malachi 2:15 Did he not make you one, although he had the residue of the Spirit? Why one? He sought godly offspring. Therefore take heed to your spirit, and let no one deal treacherously against the wife of his youth.

Malachi 2:16 "One who hates and divorces", says Yahweh, the God of Israel, "covers his garment with violence!" says Yahweh of Armies. "Therefore pay attention to your spirit, that you don't be unfaithful."

Matthew 26:41 "Watch and pray, that you don't enter into temptation. The spirit indeed is willing, but the flesh is weak."

Mark 8:12 He sighed deeply in his spirit, and said, "Why does this generation seek a sign? Most certainly I tell you, no sign will be given to this generation."

Mark 14:38 "Watch and pray, that you may not enter into temptation. The spirit indeed is willing, but the flesh is weak."

Luke 1:47 My spirit has rejoiced in God my Savior,

Luke 1:80 The child was growing and becoming strong in spirit, and was in the desert until the day of his public appearance to Israel.

Luke 2:40 The child was growing, and was becoming strong in spirit, being filled with wisdom, and the grace of God was upon him.

Luke 8:55 Her spirit returned, and she rose up immediately. He commanded that something be given to her to eat.

John 3:6 That which is born of the flesh is flesh. That which is born of the Spirit is spirit.

John 4:23 But the hour comes, and now is, when the true worshipers will worship the Father in spirit and truth, for the Father seeks such to be his worshipers.

Acts 7:59 They stoned Stephen as he called out, saying, "Lord Jesus, receive my spirit!"

Acts 17:16 Now while Paul waited for them at Athens, his spirit was provoked within him as he saw the city full of idols.

Acts 18:25 This man had been instructed in the way of the Lord; and being fervent in spirit, he spoke and taught accurately the things concerning Jesus, although he knew only the baptism of John.

Romans 1:9 For God is my witness, whom I serve in my spirit in the Good News of his Son, how unceasingly I make mention of you always in my prayers,

Romans 8:10 If Christ is in you, the body is dead because of sin, but the spirit is alive because of righteousness.

Romans 8:16 The Spirit himself testifies with our spirit that we are children of God;

1 Corinthians 2:11 For who among men knows the things of a man, except the spirit of the man, which is in him? Even so, no one knows the things of God, except God's Spirit.

1 Corinthians 5:4 In the name of our Lord Jesus Christ, you being gathered together, and my spirit, with the power of our Lord Jesus Christ,

1 Corinthians 5:5 ...are to deliver such a one to Satan for the destruction of the flesh, that the spirit may be saved in the day of the Lord Jesus.

1 Corinthians 6:17 But he who is joined to the Lord is one spirit.

1 Corinthians 6:19-20 Or don't you know that your body is a temple of the Holy Spirit who is in you, whom you have from God? You are not your own, for you were bought with a price. Therefore glorify God in your body and in your spirit, which are God's.

1 Corinthians 7:34 There is also a difference between a wife and a virgin. The unmarried woman cares about the things of the Lord, that she may be holy both in body and in spirit. But she who is married cares about the things of the world—how she may please her husband.

1 Corinthians 14:14 For if I pray in another language, my spirit prays, but my understanding is unfruitful.

1 Corinthians 14:15 What is it then? I will pray with the spirit, and I will pray with the understanding also. I will sing with the spirit, and I will sing with the understanding also.

1 Corinthians 14:16 Otherwise if you bless with the spirit, how will he who fills the place of the unlearned say the "Amen" at your giving of thanks, seeing he doesn't know what you say?

1 Corinthians 14:32 The spirits of the prophets are subject to the prophets,

1 Corinthians 15:45 So also it is written, "The first man, Adam, became a living soul." The last Adam became a life-giving spirit.

1 Corinthians 16:18 For they refreshed my spirit and yours. Therefore acknowledge those who are like that.

2 Corinthians 2:13 I had no relief for my spirit, because I didn't find Titus, my brother, but taking my leave of them, I went out into Macedonia.

2 Corinthians 7:1 Having therefore these promises, beloved, let's cleanse ourselves from all defilement of flesh and spirit, perfecting holiness in the fear of God.

2 Corinthians 7:13 Therefore we have been comforted. In our comfort we rejoiced the more exceedingly for the joy of Titus, because his spirit has been refreshed by you all.

2 Corinthians 12:18 I exhorted Titus, and I sent the brother with him. Did Titus take any advantage of you? Didn't we walk in the same spirit? Didn't we walk in the same steps?

Galatians 6:18 The grace of our Lord Jesus Christ be with your spirit, brothers. Amen.

Ephesians 4:23 ...and that you be renewed in the spirit of your mind,

Philippians 1:27 Only let your way of life be worthy of the Good News of Christ, that whether I come and see you or am absent, I may hear of your state, that you stand firm in one spirit, with one soul striving for the faith of the Good News;

Colossians 2:5 For though I am absent in the flesh, yet I am with you in the spirit, rejoicing and seeing your order, and the steadfastness of your faith in Christ.

1 Thessalonians 5:23 May the God of peace himself sanctify you completely. May your whole spirit, soul, and body be preserved blameless at the coming of our Lord Jesus Christ.

2 Thessalonians 2:2 ...not to be quickly shaken in your mind, and not be troubled, either by spirit, or by word, or by letter as if from us, saying that the day of Christ has already come.

Philemon 1:25 The grace of our Lord Jesus Christ be with your spirit. Amen.

1 Timothy 4:12 Let no man despise your youth; but be an example to those who believe, in word, in your way of life, in love, in spirit, in faith, and in purity.

2 Timothy 4:22 The Lord Jesus Christ be with your spirit. Grace be with you. Amen.

Hebrews 4:12 For the word of God is living and active, and sharper than any two-edged sword, piercing even to the dividing of soul and spirit, of both joints and marrow, and is able to discern the thoughts and intentions of the heart.

Hebrews 12:9 Furthermore, we had the fathers of our flesh to chasten us, and we paid them respect. Shall we not much rather be in subjection to the Father of spirits, and live?

Hebrews 12:23 ...to the festal gathering and assembly of the firstborn who are enrolled in heaven, to God the Judge of all, to the spirits of just men made perfect,

1 Peter 3:4 ...but in the hidden person of the heart, in the incorruptible adornment of a gentle and quiet spirit, which is very precious in the sight of God.

1 Peter 3:19 ...in whom he also went and preached to the spirits in prison,

1 Peter 4:6 For to this end the Good News was preached even to the dead, that they might be judged indeed as men in the flesh, but live as to God in the spirit.

Revelation 22:6 He said to me, "These words are faithful and true. The Lord God of the spirits of the prophets sent his angel to show to his bondservants the things which must happen soon."

Spirits of Darkness

Evil Spirit, Devil, Satan, Antichrist Spirit, Spirit of the World

Exodus 6:9 Moses spoke so to the children of Israel, but they didn't listen to Moses for anguish of spirit, and for cruel bondage.

Judges 9:23 Then God sent an evil spirit between Abimelech and the men of Shechem; and the men of Shechem dealt treacherously with Abimelech,

1 Samuel 16:14 Now Yahweh's Spirit departed from Saul, and an evil spirit from Yahweh troubled him.

1 Samuel 16:16 "Let our lord now command your servants who are in front of you to seek out a man who is a skillful player on the harp. Then when the evil spirit from God is on you, he will play with his hand, and you will be well."

1 Samuel 16:23 When the spirit from God was on Saul, David took the harp and played with his hand; so Saul was refreshed and was well, and the evil spirit departed from him.

1 Samuel 18:10 On the next day, an evil spirit from God came mightily on Saul, and he prophesied in the middle of the house. David played with his hand, as he did day by day. Saul had his spear in his hand;

1 Samuel 19:9 An evil spirit from Yahweh was on Saul, as he sat in his house with his spear in his hand; and David was playing with his hand.

Job 4:15 Then a spirit passed before my face. The hair of my flesh stood up.

Matthew 12:45 "Then he goes and takes with himself seven other spirits more evil than he is, and they enter in and dwell there. The last state of that man becomes worse than the first. Even so will it be also to this evil generation."

Luke 7:21 In that hour he cured many of diseases and plagues and evil spirits; and to many who were blind he gave sight.

Luke 8:2 ...and certain women who had been healed of evil spirits and infirmities: Mary who was called Magdalene, from whom seven demons had gone out;

Luke 9:55 But he turned and rebuked them, "You don't know of what kind of spirit you are."

Luke 11:26 "Then he goes, and takes seven other spirits more evil than himself, and they enter in and dwell there. The last state of that man becomes worse than the first."

Acts 5:3 But Peter said, "Ananias, why has Satan filled your heart to lie to the Holy Spirit and to keep back part of the price of the land?"

Acts 16:18 She was doing this for many days. But Paul, becoming greatly annoyed, turned and said to the spirit, "I command you in the name of Jesus

Christ to come out of her!" It came out that very hour."

Acts 19:13 But some of the itinerant Jews, exorcists, took on themselves to invoke over those who had the evil spirits the name of the Lord Jesus, saying, "We adjure you by Jesus whom Paul preaches."

Acts 19:16 The man in whom the evil spirit was leaped on them, overpowered them, and prevailed against them, so that they fled out of that house naked and wounded.

1 Corinthians 2:12 But we received not the spirit of the world, but the Spirit which is from God, that we might know the things that were freely given to us by God.

Ephesians 2:2 ...in which you once walked according to the course of this world, according to the prince of the power of the air, the spirit who now works in the children of disobedience.

1 Timothy 4:1 But the Spirit says expressly that in later times some will fall away from the faith, paying attention to seducing spirits and doctrines of demons,

2 Timothy 1:7 For God didn't give us a spirit of fear, but of power, love, and self-control.

1 John 4:1 Beloved, don't believe every spirit, but test the spirits, whether they are of God, because many false prophets have gone out into the world.

1 John 4:3 ...and every spirit who doesn't confess that Jesus Christ has come in the flesh is not of God, and this is the spirit of the Antichrist, of whom you have heard that it comes. Now it is in the world already.

Revelation 12:9 The great dragon was thrown down, the old serpent, he who is called the devil and Satan, the deceiver of the whole world. He was thrown down to the earth, and his angels were thrown down with him.

Revelation 16:14 ...for they are spirits of demons, performing signs; which go out to the kings of the whole inhabited earth, to gather them together for the war of that great day of God, the Almighty.

*Specific spirits
mentioned
in God's Word*

Spirit of...

Spirit of Adoption

Romans 8:15 For you didn't receive the spirit of bondage again to fear, but you received the Spirit of adoption, by whom we cry, "Abba! Father!"

Galatians 4:6 And because you are children, God sent out the Spirit of his Son into your hearts, crying, "Abba, Father!"

Spirit of Anger

Ecclesiastes 7:9 Don't be hasty in your spirit to be angry, for anger rests in the bosom of fools.

Spirit of the Antichrist

1 John 4:3 ...and every spirit who doesn't confess that Jesus Christ has come in the flesh is not of God, and this is the spirit of the Antichrist, of whom you have heard that it comes. Now it is in the world already.

Spirit of Bondage

Romans 8:15 For you didn't receive the spirit of bondage again to fear, but you received the Spirit of adoption, by whom we cry, "Abba! Father!"

Spirit of Burning

Isaiah 4:4 ...when the Lord shall have washed away the filth of the daughters of Zion, and shall have purged the blood of Jerusalem from within it, by the spirit of justice and by the spirit of burning.

Spirit of Christ

Romans 8:9 But you are not in the flesh but in the Spirit, if it is so that the Spirit of God dwells in you. But if any man doesn't have the Spirit of Christ, he is not his.

Philippians 1:19-20 For I know that this will turn out to my salvation, through your prayers and the supply of the Spirit of Jesus Christ, according to my earnest expectation and hope, that I will in no way be disappointed, but with all boldness, as always, now also Christ will be magnified in my body, whether by life or by death.

Spirit of Counsel and Might

Isaiah 11:2 Yahweh's Spirit will rest on him: the spirit of wisdom and understanding, the spirit of counsel and might, the spirit of knowledge and of the fear of Yahweh.

Spirit of Deep Sleep

Isaiah 29:10 For Yahweh has poured out on you a spirit of deep sleep, and has closed your eyes, the prophets; and he has covered your heads, the seers.

Spirit of Demons

Revelation 16:13-14 I saw coming out of the mouth of the dragon, and out of the mouth of the beast, and out of the mouth of the false prophet, three unclean spirits, something like frogs; for they are spirits of demons, performing signs; which go out to the kings of the whole inhabited earth, to gather them together for the war of that great day of God, the Almighty.

Spirit of Divination

Acts 16:16 As we were going to prayer, a certain girl having a spirit of divination met us, who brought her masters much gain by fortune telling.

Acts 16:18 She was doing this for many days. But Paul, becoming greatly annoyed, turned and said to the spirit, "I command you in the name of Jesus Christ to come out of her!" It came out that very hour.

Spirit of the Egyptians

Isaiah 19:3 The spirit of the Egyptians will fail within them. I will destroy their counsel. They will seek the idols, the charmers, those who have familiar spirits, and the wizards.

Spirit of Elijah

2 Kings 2:9 When they had gone over, Elijah said to Elisha, "Ask what I shall do for you, before I am taken from you." Elisha said, "Please let a double portion of your spirit be on me."

2 Kings 2:15 When the sons of the prophets who were at Jericho facing him saw him, they said, "The spirit of Elijah rests on Elisha." They came to meet him, and bowed themselves to the ground before him.

Luke 1:17 "He will go before him in the spirit and power of Elijah, 'to turn the hearts of the fathers to the children,' and the disobedient to the wisdom of the just; to prepare a people prepared for the Lord."

Spirit of Error

1 John 4:6 We are of God. He who knows God listens to us. He who is not of God doesn't listen to us. By this we know the spirit of truth, and the spirit of error.

Spirit of Falsehood

Micah 2:11 If a man walking in a spirit of falsehood lies: "I will prophesy to you of wine and of strong drink;" he would be the prophet of this people.

Spirit of Fear

Isaiah 11:2 Yahweh's Spirit will rest on him: the spirit of wisdom and understanding, the spirit of counsel and might, the spirit of knowledge and of the fear of Yahweh.

2 Timothy 1:7 For God didn't give us a spirit of fear, but of power, love, and self-control.

Spirit of Gentleness

1 Corinthians 4:21 What do you want? Shall I come to you with a rod, or in love and a spirit of gentleness?

Galatians 6:1 Brothers, even if a man is caught in some fault, you who are spiritual must restore such a one in a spirit of gentleness; looking to yourself so that you also aren't tempted.

Spirit of Glory

1 Peter 4:14 If you are insulted for the name of Christ, you are blessed; because the Spirit of glory and of God rests on you. On their part he is blasphemed, but on your part he is glorified.

Spirit of God

Genesis 41:38 Pharaoh said to his servants, "Can we find such a one as this, a man in whom is the Spirit of God?"

Exodus 31:3 I have filled him with the Spirit of God, in wisdom, and in understanding, and in knowledge, and in all kinds of workmanship,

Exodus 35:31 He has filled him with the Spirit of God, in wisdom, in understanding, in knowledge, and in all kinds of workmanship;

Numbers 24:2 Balaam lifted up his eyes, and he saw Israel dwelling according to their tribes; and the Spirit of God came on him.

1 Samuel 10:10 When they came there to the hill, behold, a band of prophets met him; and the Spirit of God came mightily on him, and he prophesied among them.

2 Chronicles 15:1-2 The Spirit of God came on Azariah the son of Oded: and he went out to meet Asa, and said to him, "Hear me, Asa, and all Judah and Benjamin! Yahweh is with you, while you are with him; and if you seek him, he will be found by you; but if you forsake him, he will forsake you."

2 Chronicles 24:20 The Spirit of God came on Zechariah the son of Jehoiada the priest; and he stood above the people, and said to them, "God says, 'Why do you disobey Yahweh's commandments, so that you can't prosper? Because you have forsaken Yahweh, he has also forsaken you.'"

Job 27:2-4 "As God lives, who has taken away my right, the Almighty, who has made my soul bitter (for the length of my life is still in me, and the spirit of God is in my nostrils); surely my lips will not speak unrighteousness, neither will my tongue utter deceit."

Job 33:4 The Spirit of God has made me, and the breath of the Almighty gives me life.

Ezekiel 11:24 The Spirit lifted me up, and brought me in the vision by the Spirit of God into Chaldea, to the captives. So the vision that I had seen went up from me.

Matthew 3:16 Jesus, when he was baptized, went up directly from the water: and behold, the heavens were opened to him. He saw the Spirit of God descending as a dove, and coming on him.

Matthew 12:28 But if I by the Spirit of God cast out demons, then God's Kingdom has come upon you.

Romans 8:9 But you are not in the flesh but in the Spirit, if it is so that the Spirit of God dwells in you. But if any man doesn't have the Spirit of Christ, he is not his.

1 Corinthians 6:11 Some of you were such, but you were washed. But you were sanctified. But you were justified in the name of the Lord Jesus, and in the Spirit of our God.

1 John 4:2 By this you know the Spirit of God: every spirit who confesses that Jesus Christ has come in the flesh is of God,

Revelation 3:1 And to the angel of the assembly in Sardis write: "He who has the seven Spirits of God and the seven stars says these things: "I know your works, that you have a reputation of being alive, but you are dead."

Revelation 4:5 Out of the throne proceed lightnings, sounds, and thunders. There were seven lamps of fire burning before his throne, which are the seven Spirits of God.

Revelation 5:6 I saw in the middle of the throne and of the four living creatures, and in the middle of the elders, a Lamb standing, as though it had been slain, having seven horns and seven eyes, which are the seven Spirits of God, sent out into all the earth.

Spirit of Grace and Supplication

Zechariah 12:10 I will pour on David's house, and on the inhabitants of Jerusalem, the spirit of grace and of supplication; and they will look to me whom they have pierced; and they shall mourn for him, as one mourns for his only son, and will grieve bitterly for him, as one grieves for his firstborn.

Hebrews 10:29 How much worse punishment do you think he will be judged worthy of who has trodden under foot the Son of God, and has counted the blood of the covenant with which he was sanctified an unholy thing, and has insulted the Spirit of grace?

Spirit of Heaviness

Isaiah 61:3 ...to provide for those who mourn in Zion, to give to them a garland for ashes, the oil of joy for mourning, the garment of praise for the spirit of heaviness, that they may be called trees of righteousness, the planting of Yahweh, that he may be glorified.

Spirit of Holiness

Romans 1:4 ...who was declared to be the Son of God with power, according to the Spirit of holiness, by the resurrection from the dead, Jesus Christ our Lord,

Spirit of Impurity

Zechariah 13:2 It will come to pass in that day, says Yahweh of Armies, that I will cut off the names of the idols out of the land, and they will be remembered no more. I will also cause the prophets and the spirit of impurity to pass out of the land.

Spirit of Infirmity

Luke 13:11 Behold, there was a woman who had a spirit of infirmity eighteen years. She was bent over, and could in no way straighten herself up.

Luke 13:12 When Jesus saw her, he called her, and said to her, "Woman, you are freed from your infirmity."

Spirit of Jealousy

Numbers 5:14 ...and the spirit of jealousy comes on him, and he is jealous of his wife and she is defiled; or if the spirit of jealousy comes on him, and he is jealous of his wife and she isn't defiled;

Numbers 5:30 ...or when the spirit of jealousy comes on a man, and he is jealous of his wife; then he shall set the woman before Yahweh, and the priest shall execute on her all this law.

Ezekiel 8:3 He stretched out the form of a hand, and took me by a lock of my head; and the Spirit lifted me up between earth and the sky, and brought me in the visions of God to Jerusalem, to the door of the gate of the inner court that looks toward the north; where there was the seat of the image of jealousy, which provokes to jealousy.

Spirit of Justice

Isaiah 4:4 ...when the Lord shall have washed away the filth of the daughters of Zion, and shall have purged the blood of Jerusalem from within it, by the spirit of justice and by the spirit of burning.

Isaiah 28:6 ...and a spirit of justice to him who sits in judgment, and strength to those who turn back the battle at the gate.

Spirit of Knowledge

Isaiah 11:2 Yahweh's Spirit will rest on him: the spirit of wisdom and understanding, the spirit of counsel and might, the spirit of knowledge and of the fear of Yahweh.

Colossians 1:9 For this cause, we also, since the day we heard this, don't cease praying and making requests for you, that you may be filled with the knowledge of his will in all spiritual wisdom and understanding,

Spirit of Legalism

Romans 2:29 ...but he is a Jew who is one inwardly, and circumcision is that of the heart, in the spirit not in the letter; whose praise is not from men, but from God.

Romans 7:6 But now we have been discharged from the law, having died to that in which we were held; so that we serve in newness of the spirit, and not in oldness of the letter.

Romans 8:4 that the ordinance of the law might be fulfilled in us, who walk not after the flesh, but after the Spirit.

2 Corinthians 3:6 ...who also made us sufficient as servants of a new covenant, not of the letter, but of the Spirit. For the letter kills, but the Spirit gives life.

Spirit of Life

Genesis 7:22 All on the dry land, in whose nostrils was the breath of the spirit of life, died.

Romans 8:2 For the law of the Spirit of life in Christ Jesus made me free from the law of sin and of death.

2 Corinthians 3:6 ...who also made us sufficient as servants of a new covenant, not of the letter, but of the Spirit. For the letter kills, but the Spirit gives life.

Spirit of the Philistines

2 Chronicles 21:16 Yahweh stirred up against Jehoram the spirit of the Philistines, and of the Arabians who are beside the Ethiopians;

Spirit of Perverseness

Isaiah 19:14 Yahweh has mixed a spirit of perverseness in the middle of her; and they have caused Egypt to go astray in all of its works, like a drunken man staggers in his vomit.

Spirit of Pride

Ecclesiastes 7:8 Better is the end of a thing than its beginning. The patient in spirit is better than the proud in spirit.

Ecclesiastes 10:4 If the spirit of the ruler rises up against you, don't leave your place; for gentleness lays great offenses to rest.

Spirit of Prophecy

Revelation 19:10 I fell down before his feet to worship him. He said to me, "Look! Don't do it! I am a fellow bondservant with you and with your brothers who hold the testimony of Jesus. Worship God, for the testimony of Jesus is the Spirit of Prophecy."

Spirit of Prostitution

Hosea 4:12 My people consult with their wooden idol, and answer to a stick of wood. Indeed the spirit of prostitution has led them astray, and they have been unfaithful to their God.

Hosea 5:4 Their deeds won't allow them to turn to their God; for the spirit of prostitution is within them, and they don't know Yahweh.

Spirit of Stupor

Deuteronomy 29:4 But Yahweh has not given you a heart to know, eyes to see, and ears to hear, to this day.

Romans 11:8 According as it is written, "God gave them a spirit of stupor, eyes that they should not see, and ears that they should not hear, to this very day."

Spirit of the Lord

Luke 4:18 "The Spirit of the Lord is on me, because he has anointed me to preach good news to the poor. He has sent me to heal the broken hearted, to proclaim release to the captives, recovering of sight to the blind, to deliver those who are crushed,"

Acts 5:9 But Peter asked her, "How is it that you have agreed together to tempt the Spirit of the Lord? Behold, the feet of those who have buried your husband are at the door, and they will carry you out."

2 Corinthians 3:17 Now the Lord is the Spirit and where the Spirit of the Lord is, there is liberty.

Spirit of Truth

John 14:17 ...the Spirit of truth, whom the world can't receive; for it doesn't see him and doesn't know him. You know him, for he lives with you, and will be in you.

John 15:26 "When the Counselor has come, whom I will send to you from the Father, the Spirit of truth, who proceeds from the Father, he will testify about me."

John 16:13 However when he, the Spirit of truth, has come, he will guide you into all truth, for he will not speak from himself; but whatever he hears, he will speak. He will declare to you things that are coming.

1 John 4:6 We are of God. He who knows God listens to us. He who is not of God doesn't listen to us. By this we know the spirit of truth, and the spirit of error.

Spirit of Wisdom

Exodus 28:3 You shall speak to all who are wise-hearted, whom I have filled with the spirit of wisdom, that they make Aaron's garments to sanctify him, that he may minister to me in the priest's office.

Deuteronomy 34:9 Joshua the son of Nun was full of the spirit of wisdom, for Moses had laid his hands on him. The children of Israel listened to him, and did as Yahweh commanded Moses.

Isaiah 11:2 Yahweh's Spirit will rest on him: the spirit of wisdom and understanding, the spirit of counsel and might, the spirit of knowledge and of the fear of Yahweh.

Ephesians 1:17 ...that the God of our Lord Jesus Christ, the Father of glory, may give to you a spirit of wisdom and revelation in the knowledge of him,

*More spirits
mentioned
in God's Word*

More Spirits..

Anguish of Spirit

Exodus 6:9 Moses spoke so to the children of Israel, but they didn't listen to Moses for anguish of spirit, and for cruel bondage.

Job 7:11 "Therefore I will not keep silent. I will speak in the anguish of my spirit. I will complain in the bitterness of my soul."

Isaiah 65:14 Behold, my servants will sing for joy of heart, but you will cry for sorrow of heart, and will wail for anguish of spirit.

Arrogant Spirit

Proverbs 16:18 Pride goes before destruction, and an arrogant spirit before a fall.

Broken Spirit

Psalm 51:17 The sacrifices of God are a broken spirit. O God, you will not despise a broken and contrite heart.

Contrite Spirit

Isaiah 66:2 "For my hand has made all these things, and so all these things came to be," says Yahweh: "but I will look to this man, even to he who is poor and of a contrite spirit, and who trembles at my word."

Crushed Spirit

Proverbs 17:22 A cheerful heart makes good medicine, but a crushed spirit dries up the bones.

Proverbs 18:14 A man's spirit will sustain him in sickness, but a crushed spirit, who can bear?

Psalm 34:18 Yahweh is near to those who have a broken heart, and saves those who have a crushed spirit.

Luke 4:18 "The Spirit of the Lord is on me, because he has anointed me to preach good news to the poor. He has sent me to heal the broken hearted, to proclaim release to the captives, recovering of sight to the blind, to deliver those who are crushed,"

Departed Spirits

Job 26:5 "The departed spirits tremble, those beneath the waters and all that live in them."

Psalm 88:10 Do you show wonders to the dead? Do the departed spirits rise up and praise you? Selah.

Proverbs 2:18 ...for her house leads down to death, her paths to the departed spirits.

Proverbs 9:18 But he doesn't know that the departed spirits are there, that her guests are in the depths of Sheol.

Proverbs 21:16 The man who wanders out of the way of understanding shall rest in the assembly of the departed spirits.

Isaiah 14:9 Sheol from beneath has moved for you to meet you at your coming. It stirs up the departed spirits for you, even all the rulers of the earth. It has raised up from their thrones all the kings of the nations.

Isaiah 26:14 The dead shall not live. The departed spirits shall not rise. Therefore you have visited and destroyed them, and caused all memory of them to perish.

Isaiah 26:19 Your dead shall live. My dead bodies shall arise. Awake and sing, you who dwell in the dust; for your dew is like the dew of herbs, and the earth will cast out the departed spirits.

Excellent Spirit

Daniel 5:12 "...because an excellent spirit, knowledge, understanding, interpreting of dreams, showing of dark sentences, and dissolving of doubts were found in the same Daniel, whom the king named Belteshazzar. Now let Daniel be called, and he will show the interpretation."

Daniel 6:3 Then this Daniel was distinguished above the presidents and the local governors, because an excellent spirit was in him; and the king thought to set him over the whole realm.

Familiar Spirit

1 Samuel 28:3 Now Samuel was dead, and all Israel had mourned for him, and buried him in Ramah, even in his own city. Saul had sent away those who had familiar spirits and the wizards out of the land.

1 Samuel 28:7 Then Saul said to his servants, "Seek for me a woman who has a familiar spirit, that I may go to her, and inquire of her." His servants said to him, "Behold, there is a woman who has a familiar spirit at Endor."

1 Samuel 28:9 The woman said to him, "Behold, you know what Saul has done, how he has cut off those who have familiar spirits and the wizards out of the land. Why then do you lay a snare for my life, to cause me to die?"

2 Kings 23:24 Moreover Josiah removed those who had familiar spirits, the wizards, and the teraphim, and the idols, and all the abominations that were seen in the land of Judah and in Jerusalem, that he might confirm the words of the law which were written in the book that Hilkiah the priest found in Yahweh's house.

1 Chronicles 10:13 So Saul died for his trespass which he committed against Yahweh, because of Yahweh's word, which he didn't keep; and also because he asked counsel of one who had a familiar spirit, to inquire,

2 Chronicles 33:6 He also made his children to pass through the fire in the valley of the son of Hinnom. He practiced sorcery, divination, and witchcraft, and dealt with those who had familiar spirits and with wizards. He did much evil in Yahweh's sight, to provoke him to anger.

Isaiah 8:19 When they tell you, "Consult with those who have familiar spirits and with the wizards, who chirp and who mutter," shouldn't a people consult with their God? Should they consult the dead on behalf of the living?

Isaiah 19:3 The spirit of the Egyptians will fail within them. I will destroy their counsel. They will seek the idols, the charmers, those who have familiar spirits, and the wizards.

Isaiah 29:4 You will be brought down, and will speak out of the ground. Your speech will mumble out of the dust. Your voice will be as of one who has a familiar spirit, out of the ground, and your speech will whisper out of the dust.

Fervent in Spirit

Acts 18:25 This man had been instructed in the way of the Lord; and being fervent in spirit, he spoke and taught accurately the things concerning Jesus, although he knew only the baptism of John.

Romans 12:11 ...not lagging in diligence; fervent in spirit; serving the Lord;

1 Peter 1:22 Seeing you have purified your souls in your obedience to the truth through the Spirit in sincere brotherly affection, love one another from the heart fervently,

Fruit of the Spirit

Romans 8:23 Not only so, but ourselves also, who have the first fruits of the Spirit, even we ourselves groan within ourselves, waiting for adoption, the redemption of our body.

Galatians 5:22-23 But the fruit of the Spirit is love, joy, peace, patience, kindness, goodness, faith, gentleness, and self-control. Against such things there is no law.

Ephesians 5:9-10 ...for the fruit of the Spirit is in all goodness and righteousness and truth, proving what is well pleasing to the Lord.

Gentle and Quiet Spirit

1 Peter 3:4 ...but in the hidden person of the heart, in the incorruptible adornment of a gentle and quiet spirit, which is very precious in the sight of God.

Grieved in Spirit

Isaiah 54:6 "For Yahweh has called you as a wife forsaken and grieved in spirit, even a wife of youth, when she is cast off," says your God.

Daniel 7:15 "As for me, Daniel, my spirit was grieved within my body, and the visions of my head troubled me."

Humble Spirit/Lowly Spirit

Proverbs 16:19 It is better to be of a lowly spirit with the poor, than to divide the plunder with the proud.

Proverbs 29:23 A man's pride brings him low, but one of lowly spirit gains honor.

Isaiah 57:15 For the high and lofty One who inhabits eternity, whose name is Holy, says: "I dwell in the high and holy place, with him also who is of a contrite and humble spirit, to revive the spirit of the humble, and to revive the heart of the contrite."

Matthew 5:3 "Blessed are the poor in spirit, for theirs is the Kingdom of Heaven."

Lying Spirit

1 Kings 22:22 Yahweh said to him, 'How?' He said, 'I will go out and will be a lying spirit in the mouth of all his prophets.' He said, 'You will entice him, and will also prevail. Go out and do so.'

1 Kings 22:23 "Now therefore, behold, Yahweh has put a lying spirit in the mouth of all these your prophets; and Yahweh has spoken evil concerning you."

2 Chronicles 18:21 "He said, 'I will go, and will be a lying spirit in the mouth of all his prophets.' "He said, 'You will entice him, and will prevail also. Go and do so.'"

2 Chronicles 18:22 "Now therefore, behold, Yahweh has put a lying spirit in the mouth of these your prophets; and Yahweh has spoken evil concerning you."

Mute Spirit

Mark 9:17 One of the multitude answered, "Teacher, I brought to you my son, who has a mute spirit;"

Mark 9:25 When Jesus saw that a multitude came running together, he rebuked the unclean spirit, saying to him, "You mute and deaf spirit, I command you, come out of him, and never enter him again!"

Religious Spirit

Acts 23:8 For the Sadducees say that there is no resurrection, nor angel, nor spirit; but the Pharisees confess all of these.

Seducing Spirits

1 Timothy 4:1 But the Spirit says expressly that in later times some will fall away from the faith, paying attention to seducing spirits and doctrines of demons,

Serving Spirits (Ministering Spirits, Angels)

Hebrews 1:14 Aren't they all serving spirits, sent out to do service for the sake of those who will inherit salvation?

Troubled in Spirit

Genesis 41:8 In the morning, his spirit was troubled, and he sent and called for all of Egypt's magicians and wise men. Pharaoh told them his dreams, but there was no one who could interpret them to Pharaoh.

Daniel 2:1 In the second year of the reign of Nebuchadnezzar, Nebuchadnezzar dreamed dreams; and his spirit was troubled, and his sleep went from him.

John 11:33 When Jesus therefore saw her weeping, and the Jews weeping who came with her, he groaned in the spirit, and was troubled,

John 13:21 When Jesus had said this, he was troubled in spirit, and testified, "Most certainly I tell you that one of you will betray me."

Trustworthy Spirit

Proverbs 11:13 One who brings gossip betrays a confidence, but one who is of a trustworthy spirit is one who keeps a secret.

Unclean Spirit

Matthew 10:1 He called to himself his twelve disciples, and gave them authority over unclean spirits, to cast them out, and to heal every disease and every sickness.

Matthew 12:43 "When an unclean spirit has gone out of a man, he passes through waterless places seeking rest, and doesn't find it."

Mark 1:26 The unclean spirit, convulsing him and crying with a loud voice, came out of him.

Mark 3:11 The unclean spirits, whenever they saw him, fell down before him and cried, "You are the Son of God!"

Mark 5:2 When he had come out of the boat, immediately a man with an unclean spirit met him out of the tombs.

Mark 5:8 For he said to him, "Come out of the man, you unclean spirit!"

Mark 5:13 At once Jesus gave them permission. The unclean spirits came out and entered into the pigs. The herd of about two thousand rushed down the steep bank into the sea, and they were drowned in the sea.

Mark 7:25 For a woman, whose little daughter had an unclean spirit, having heard of him, came and fell down at his feet.

Mark 9:25 When Jesus saw that a multitude came running together, he rebuked the unclean spirit, saying to him, "You mute and deaf spirit, I command you, come out of him, and never enter him again!"

Luke 4:33 In the synagogue there was a man who had a spirit of an unclean demon, and he cried out with a loud voice,

Luke 8:29 For Jesus was commanding the unclean spirit to come out of the man. For the unclean spirit had often seized the man. He was kept under guard, and bound with chains and fetters. Breaking the bonds apart, he was driven by the demon into the desert.

Luke 11:24 The unclean spirit, when he has gone out of the man, passes through dry places, seeking rest, and finding none, he says, 'I will turn back to my house from which I came out.'

Acts 8:7 For unclean spirits came out of many of those who had them. They came out, crying with a loud voice. Many who had been paralyzed and lame were healed.

Revelation 16:13 I saw coming out of the mouth of the dragon, and out of the mouth of the beast, and out of the mouth of the false prophet, three unclean spirits, something like frogs;

Revelation 18:2 He cried with a mighty voice, saying, "Fallen, fallen is Babylon the great, and she has become a habitation of demons, a prison of every unclean spirit, and a prison of every unclean and hateful bird!"

Willing Spirit

Exodus 35:21 They came, everyone whose heart stirred him up, and everyone whom his spirit made willing, and brought Yahweh's offering for the work of the Tent of Meeting, and for all of its service, and for the holy garments.

Psalm 51:12 Restore to me the joy of your salvation. Uphold me with a willing spirit.

Matthew 26:41 "Watch and pray, that you don't enter into temptation. The spirit indeed is willing, but the flesh is weak."

Mark 14:38 "Watch and pray, that you may not enter into temptation. The spirit indeed is willing, but the flesh is weak."

Verses with "Spiritual"
or "Spiritually"

Spiritual, Spiritually

Blessing, Discernment, Forces, Gifts, Rock, Sacrifices, Service, Songs, Wisdom

Romans 12:1 Therefore I urge you, brothers, by the mercies of God, to present your bodies a living sacrifice, holy, acceptable to God, which is your spiritual service.

Romans 15:27 Yes, it has been their good pleasure, and they are their debtors. For if the Gentiles have been made partakers of their spiritual things, they owe it to them also to serve them in fleshly things.

1 Corinthians 2:14 Now the natural man doesn't receive the things of God's Spirit, for they are foolishness to him, and he can't know them, because they are spiritually discerned.

1 Corinthians 10:4 ...and all drank the same spiritual drink. For they drank of a spiritual rock that followed them, and the rock was Christ.

1 Corinthians 14:12 So also you, since you are zealous for spiritual gifts, seek that you may abound to the building up of the assembly.

1 Corinthians 14:37 If any man thinks himself to be a prophet, or spiritual, let him recognize the things which I write to you, that they are the commandment of the Lord.

Galatians 6:1 Brothers, even if a man is caught in some fault, you who are spiritual must restore such a one in a spirit of gentleness; looking to yourself so that you also aren't tempted.

Ephesians 1:3 Blessed be the God and Father of our Lord Jesus Christ, who has blessed us with every spiritual blessing in the heavenly places in Christ,

Ephesians 6:12 For our wrestling is not against flesh and blood, but against the principalities, against the powers, against the world's rulers of the darkness of this age, and against the spiritual forces of wickedness in the heavenly places.

Colossians 1:9-10 For this cause, we also, since the day we heard this, don't cease praying and making requests for you, that you may be filled with the knowledge of his will in all spiritual wisdom and understanding, that you may walk worthily of the Lord, to please him in all respects, bearing fruit in every good work and increasing in the knowledge of God,

Colossians 3:16 Let the word of Christ dwell in you richly; in all wisdom teaching and admonishing one another with psalms, hymns, and spiritual songs, singing with grace in your heart to the Lord.

1 Peter 2:5 You also, as living stones, are built up as a spiritual house, to be a holy priesthood, to offer up spiritual sacrifices, acceptable to God through Jesus Christ.

Revelation 11:8 Their dead bodies will be in the street of the great city, which spiritually is called Sodom and Egypt, where also their Lord was crucified.

Waging War

Waging War

Authority, Warfare, Pray, Confess, Repent, Renounce, Release, Forgive

Genesis 4:6-7 Yahweh said to Cain, "Why are you angry? Why has the expression of your face fallen? If you do well, won't it be lifted up? If you don't do well, sin crouches at the door. Its desire is for you, but you are to rule over it."

Deuteronomy 3:22 You shall not fear them; for Yahweh your God himself fights for you.

1 Samuel 15:23 "For rebellion is as the sin of witchcraft, and stubbornness is as idolatry and teraphim. Because you have rejected Yahweh's word, he has also rejected you from being king."

2 Chronicles 7:14 ...if my people, who are called by my name, will humble themselves, pray, seek my face, and turn from their wicked ways, then I will hear from heaven, will forgive their sin, and will heal their land.

Psalm 5:4-7 For you are not a God who has pleasure in wickedness. Evil can't live with you. The arrogant will not stand in your sight. You hate all workers of iniquity. You will destroy those who speak lies. Yahweh abhors the bloodthirsty and deceitful man. But as for me, in the abundance of your loving kindness I will come into your house. I will bow toward your holy temple in reverence of you.

Psalm 9:2-3 I will be glad and rejoice in you. I will sing praise to your name, O Most High. When my enemies turn back, they stumble and perish in your presence.

Psalm 18:2 Yahweh is my rock, my fortress, and my deliverer; my God, my rock, in whom I take refuge; my shield, and the horn of my salvation, my high tower.

Psalm 32:5 I acknowledged my sin to you. I didn't hide my iniquity. I said, I will confess my transgressions to Yahweh, and you forgave the iniquity of my sin. Selah.

Psalm 44:5-6 Through you, we will push down our adversaries. Through your name, we will tread down those who rise up against us. For I will not trust in my bow, neither will my sword save me.

Psalm 86:5 For you, Lord, are good, and ready to forgive, abundant in loving kindness to all those who call on you.

Psalm 115:4-8 Their idols are silver and gold, the work of men's hands. They have mouths, but they don't speak. They have eyes, but they don't see. They have ears, but they don't hear. They have noses, but they don't smell. They have hands, but they don't feel. They have feet, but they don't walk, neither do they speak through their throat. Those who make them will be like them; yes, everyone who trusts in them.

Psalm 119:50 This is my comfort in my affliction, for your word has revived me.

Psalm 139:23-24 I acknowledged my sin to you. I didn't hide my iniquity. I said, I will confess my transgressions to Yahweh, and you forgave the iniquity of my sin. Selah.

Psalm 144:1-2 Blessed be Yahweh, my rock, who teaches my hands to war, and my fingers to battle: my loving kindness, my fortress, my high tower, my deliverer, my shield, and he in whom I take refuge, who subdues my people under me.

Psalm 149:6-9 May the high praises of God be in their mouths, and a two-edged sword in their hand, to execute vengeance on the nations, and punishments on the peoples; to bind their kings with chains, and their nobles with fetters of iron; to execute on them the written judgment. All his saints have this honor. Praise Yah!

Proverbs 6:31 ...but if he is found, he shall restore seven times. He shall give all the wealth of his house.

Proverbs 26:2 Like a fluttering sparrow, like a darting swallow, so the undeserved curse doesn't come to rest.

Ecclesiastes 12:7 ...and the dust returns to the earth as it was, and the spirit returns to God who gave it.

Isaiah 5:13-14 Therefore my people go into captivity for lack of knowledge. Their honorable men are famished, and their multitudes are parched with thirst. Therefore Sheol has enlarged its desire, and opened its mouth without measure; and their glory, their multitude, their pomp, and he who rejoices among them, descend into it.

Isaiah 9:7 Of the increase of his government and of peace there shall be no end, on David's throne, and on his kingdom, to establish it, and to uphold it with justice and with righteousness from that time on, even forever. The zeal of Yahweh of Armies will perform this.

Isaiah 41:10 Don't you be afraid, for I am with you. Don't be dismayed, for I am your God. I will strengthen you. Yes, I will help you. Yes, I will uphold you with the right hand of my righteousness.

Isaiah 43:2 When you pass through the waters, I will be with you, and through the rivers, they will not overflow you. When you walk through the fire, you will not be burned, and flame will not scorch you.

Isaiah 49:25 But Yahweh says, "Even the captives of the mighty shall be taken away, and the plunder retrieved from the fierce, for I will contend with him who contends with you and I will save your children."

Isaiah 54:17 "No weapon that is formed against you will prevail; and you will condemn every tongue that rises against you in judgment. This is the heritage of Yahweh's servants, and their righteousness is of me," says Yahweh.

Isaiah 58:12 Those who will be of you will build the old waste places. You will raise up the foundations of many generations. You will be called Repairer of the Breach, Restorer of Paths with Dwellings.

Ezekiel 20:43 There you will remember your ways, and all your deeds in which you have polluted yourselves. Then you will loathe yourselves in your own sight for all your evils that you have committed.

Joel 2:12-13 "Yet even now," says Yahweh, "turn to me with all your heart, and with fasting, and with weeping, and with mourning." Tear your heart, and not your garments, and turn to Yahweh, your God; for he is gracious and merciful, slow to anger, and abundant in loving kindness, and relents from sending calamity.

Joel 2:32 It will happen that whoever will call on Yahweh's name shall be saved; for in Mount Zion and in Jerusalem there will be those who escape, as Yahweh has said, and among the remnant, those whom Yahweh calls.

Matthew 3:7-8 But when he saw many of the Pharisees and Sadducees coming for his baptism, he said to them, "You offspring of vipers, who warned you to flee from the wrath to come? Therefore produce fruit worthy of repentance!"

Matthew 4:10-11 Then Jesus said to him, "Get behind me, Satan! For it is written, 'You shall worship the Lord your God, and you shall serve him only.'"

Matthew 6:14-15 "For if you forgive men their trespasses, your heavenly Father will also forgive you. But if you don't forgive men their trespasses, neither will your Father forgive your trespasses."

Matthew 11:28-30 "Come to me, all you who labor and are heavily burdened, and I will give you rest. Take my yoke upon you and learn from me, for I am gentle and humble in heart; and you will find rest for your souls. For my yoke is easy, and my burden is light."

Matthew 12:29 Or how can one enter into the house of the strong man and plunder his goods, unless he first bind the strong man? Then he will plunder his house.

Matthew 12:43-45 "When an unclean spirit has gone out of a man, he passes through waterless places seeking rest, and doesn't find it. Then he says, 'I will return into my house from which I came;' and when he has come back, he finds it empty, swept, and put in order. Then he goes and takes with himself seven other spirits more evil than he is, and they enter in and dwell there. The last state of that man becomes worse than the first. Even so will it be also to this evil generation."

Matthew 16:15 He said to them, "But who do you say that I am?"

Matthew 16:18 "I also tell you that you are Peter, and on this rock I will build my assembly, and the gates of Hades will not prevail against it."

Matthew 16:19 "I will give to you the keys of the Kingdom of Heaven, and whatever you bind on earth will have been bound in heaven; and whatever you release on earth will have been released in heaven."

Mark 1:23-26 Immediately there was in their synagogue a man with an unclean spirit, and he cried out, saying, "Ha! What do we have to do with you, Jesus, you Nazarene? Have you come to destroy us? I know you who you are: the Holy One of God!" Jesus rebuked him, saying, "Be quiet, and come out of him!" The unclean spirit, convulsing him and crying with a loud voice, came out of him.

Mark 5:19-20 He didn't allow him, but said to him, "Go to your house, to your friends, and tell them what great things the Lord has done for you, and how he had mercy on you." He went his way, and began to proclaim in Decapolis how Jesus had done great things for him, and everyone marveled.

Mark 6:31 He said to them, "You come apart into a deserted place, and rest awhile." For there were many coming and going, and they had no leisure so much as to eat.

Mark 7:24 From there he arose, and went away into the borders of Tyre and Sidon. He entered into a house, and didn't want anyone to know it, but he couldn't escape notice.

Mark 9:25 When Jesus saw that a multitude came running together, he rebuked the unclean spirit, saying to him, "You mute and deaf spirit, I command you, come out of him, and never enter him again!"

Mark 9:29 He said to them, "This kind can come out by nothing, except by prayer and fasting."

Mark 11:23 For most certainly I tell you, whoever may tell this mountain, 'Be taken up and cast into the sea,' and doesn't doubt in his heart, but believes that what he says is happening; he shall have whatever he says.

Mark 16:17-18 "These signs will accompany those who believe: in my name they will cast out demons; they will speak with new languages; they will take up serpents; and if they drink any deadly thing, it will in no way hurt them; they will lay hands on the sick, and they will recover."

Luke 1:37 For nothing spoken by God is impossible.

Luke 9:1 He called the twelve together, and gave them power and authority over all demons, and to cure diseases.

Luke 10:17-19 The seventy returned with joy, saying, "Lord, even the demons are subject to us in your name!" He said to them, "I saw Satan having fallen like lightning from heaven. Behold, I give you authority to tread on serpents and scorpions, and over all the power of the enemy. Nothing will in any way hurt you."

Luke 11:20-22 But if I by God's finger cast out demons, then God's Kingdom has come to you. "When the strong man, fully armed, guards his own dwelling, his goods are safe. But when someone stronger attacks him and overcomes him, he takes from him his whole armor in which he trusted, and divides his plunder."

Luke 12:12 ...for the Holy Spirit will teach you in that same hour what you must say.

John 3:3 Jesus answered him, "Most certainly, I tell you, unless one is born anew, he can't see God's Kingdom."

John 10:10 The thief only comes to steal, kill, and destroy. I came that they may have life, and may have it abundantly.

John 13:2-4 During supper, the devil having already put into the heart of Judas Iscariot, Simon's son, to betray him, Jesus, knowing that the Father had given all things into his hands, and that he came from God, and was going to God, arose from supper, and laid aside his outer garments. He took a towel and wrapped a towel around his waist.

John 14:30-31 I will no more speak much with you, for the prince of the world comes, and he has nothing in me. But that the world may know that I love the Father, and as the Father commanded me, even so I do. Arise, let's go from here.

John 15:10 If you keep my commandments, you will remain in my love; even as I have kept my Father's commandments, and remain in his love.

Acts 1:8 "But you will receive power when the Holy Spirit has come upon you. You will be witnesses to me in Jerusalem, in all Judea and Samaria, and to the uttermost parts of the earth."

Acts 2:4 They were all filled with the Holy Spirit, and began to speak with other languages, as the Spirit gave them the ability to speak.

Acts 9:31 So the assemblies throughout all Judea, Galilee, and Samaria had peace, and were built up. They were multiplied, walking in the fear of the Lord and in the comfort of the Holy Spirit.

Acts 10:38 ...even Jesus of Nazareth, how God anointed him with the Holy Spirit and with power, who went about doing good and healing all who were oppressed by the devil, for God was with him.

Acts 19:18-19 Many also of those who had believed came, confessing, and declaring their deeds. Many of those who practiced magical arts brought their books together and burned them in the sight of all. They counted their price, and found it to be fifty thousand pieces of silver.

Romans 6:16 Don't you know that when you present yourselves as servants and obey someone, you are the servants of whomever you obey; whether of sin to death, or of obedience to righteousness?

Romans 7:21-23 I find then the law that, to me, while I desire to do good, evil is present. For I delight in God's law after the inward person, but I see a different law in my members, warring against the law of my mind, and bringing me into captivity under the law of sin which is in my members.

Romans 8:26 In the same way, the Spirit also helps our weaknesses, for we don't know how to pray as we ought. But the Spirit himself makes intercession for us with groanings which can't be uttered.

Romans 8:37 No, in all these things, we are more than conquerors through him who loved us.

Romans 8:38–39 For I am persuaded that neither death, nor life, nor angels, nor principalities, nor things present, nor things to come, nor powers, nor height, nor depth, nor any other created thing will be able to separate us from God's love which is in Christ Jesus our Lord.

Romans 10:10 For with the heart, one believes resulting in righteousness; and with the mouth confession is made resulting in salvation.

Romans 12:10-12 In love of the brothers be tenderly affectionate to one another; in honor preferring one another; not lagging in diligence; fervent in spirit; serving the Lord; rejoicing in hope; enduring in troubles; continuing steadfastly in prayer;

Romans 14:16-17 Then don't let your good be slandered, for God's Kingdom is not eating and drinking, but righteousness, peace, and joy in the Holy Spirit.

1 Corinthians 10:13 No temptation has taken you except what is common to man. God is faithful, who will not allow you to be tempted above what you are able, but will with the temptation also make the way of escape, that you may be able to endure it.

1 Corinthians 11:27-30 Therefore whoever eats this bread or drinks the Lord's cup in a way unworthy of the Lord will be guilty of the body and the blood of the Lord. But let a man examine himself, and so let him eat of the bread, and drink of the cup. For he who eats and drinks in an unworthy way eats and drinks judgment to himself if he doesn't discern the Lord's body. For this cause many among you are weak and sickly, and not a few sleep.

1 Corinthians 12:10 ...and to another workings of miracles; and to another prophecy; and to another discerning of spirits; to another different kinds of languages; and to another the interpretation of languages.

2 Corinthians 4:2-4 But we have renounced the hidden things of shame, not walking in craftiness, nor handling the word of God deceitfully, but by the manifestation of the truth commending ourselves to every man's conscience in the sight of God. Even if our Good News is veiled, it is veiled in those who are dying, in whom the god of this world has blinded the minds of the unbelieving, that the light of the Good News of the glory of Christ, who is the image of God, should not dawn on them.

2 Corinthians 7:1 Having therefore these promises, beloved, let's cleanse ourselves from all defilement of flesh and spirit, perfecting holiness in the fear of God.

2 Corinthians 10:3-6 For though we walk in the flesh, we don't wage war according to the flesh; for the weapons of our warfare are not of the flesh, but mighty before God to the throwing down of strongholds, throwing down imaginations and every high thing that is exalted against the knowledge of God and bringing every thought into captivity to the obedience of Christ, and being in readiness to avenge all disobedience when your obedience is made full.

Galatians 5:17 For the flesh lusts against the Spirit, and the Spirit against the flesh; and these are contrary to one another, that you may not do the things that you desire.

Galatians 5:19-21 Now the deeds of the flesh are obvious, which are: adultery, sexual immorality, uncleanness, lustfulness, idolatry, sorcery, hatred, strife, jealousies, outbursts of anger, rivalries, divisions, heresies, envy, murders, drunkenness, orgies, and things like these; of which I forewarn you, even as I also forewarned you, that those who practice such things will not inherit God's Kingdom.

Ephesians 1:22-23 He put all things in subjection under his feet, and gave him to be head over all things for the assembly, which is his body, the fullness of him who fills all in all.

Ephesians 3:10–11 ...to the intent that now through the assembly the manifold wisdom of God might be made known to the principalities and the powers in the heavenly places, according to the eternal purpose which he accomplished in Christ Jesus our Lord.

Ephesians 3:19 ...and to know Christ's love which surpasses knowledge, that you may be filled with all the fullness of God.

Ephesians 4:22-24 ...that you put away, as concerning your former way of life, the old man that grows corrupt after the lusts of deceit, and that you be renewed in the spirit of your mind, and put on the new man, who in the likeness of God has been created in righteousness and holiness of truth.

Ephesians 5:15-16 Therefore watch carefully how you walk, not as unwise, but as wise, redeeming the time, because the days are evil.

Ephesians 5:25-27 Husbands, love your wives, even as Christ also loved the assembly, and gave himself up for it; that he might sanctify it, having cleansed it by the washing of water with the word, that he might present the assembly to himself gloriously, not having spot or wrinkle or any such thing; but that it should be holy and without defect.

Ephesians 6:10-13 Finally, be strong in the Lord, and in the strength of his might. Put on the whole armor of God, that you may be able to stand against the wiles of the devil. For our wrestling is not against flesh and blood, but against the principalities, against the powers, against the world's rulers of the darkness of this age, and against the spiritual forces of wickedness in the heavenly places. Therefore put on the whole armor of God, that you may be able to withstand in the evil day, and having done all, to stand.

Ephesians 6:15-16 ...and having fitted your feet with the preparation of the Good News of peace, above all, taking up the shield of faith, with which you will be able to quench all the fiery darts of the evil one.

Ephesians 6:18 ...with all prayer and requests, praying at all times in the Spirit, and being watchful to this end in all perseverance and requests for all the saints:

Philippians 1:27-28 Only let your way of life be worthy of the Good News of Christ, that whether I come and see you or am absent, I may hear of your state, that you stand firm in one spirit, with one soul striving for the faith of the Good News; and in nothing frightened by the adversaries, which is for them a proof of destruction, but to you of salvation, and that from God.

Philippians 2:12-13 So then, my beloved, even as you have always obeyed, not only in my presence, but now much more in my absence, work out your own salvation with fear and trembling. For it is God who works in you both to will and to work, for his good pleasure.

Philippians 4:8 Finally, brothers, whatever things are true, whatever things are honorable, whatever things are just, whatever things are pure, whatever things are lovely, whatever things are of good report: if there is any virtue and if there is any praise, think about these things.

Colossians 1:16 For by him all things were created in the heavens and on the earth, visible things and invisible things, whether thrones or dominions or principalities or powers. All things have been created through him and for him.

Colossians 2:15-17 Having stripped the principalities and the powers, he made a show of them openly, triumphing over them in it. Let no one therefore judge you in eating, or in drinking, or with respect to a feast day or a new moon or a

Sabbath day, which are a shadow of the things to come; but the body is Christ's.

Colossians 2:18-19 Let no one rob you of your prize by self-abasement and worshiping of the angels, dwelling in the things which he has not seen, vainly puffed up by his fleshly mind, and not holding firmly to the Head, from whom all the body, being supplied and knit together through the joints and ligaments, grows with God's growth.

1 Thessalonians 5:17 Pray without ceasing.

1 Thessalonians 5:23 May the God of peace himself sanctify you completely. May your whole spirit, soul, and body be preserved blameless at the coming of our Lord Jesus Christ.

1 Timothy 1:18 I commit this instruction to you, my child Timothy, according to the prophecies which were given to you before, that by them you may wage the good warfare,

1 Timothy 4:1 But the Spirit says expressly that in later times some will fall away from the faith, paying attention to seducing spirits and doctrines of demons,

1 Timothy 6:12 Fight the good fight of faith. Take hold of the eternal life to which you were called, and you confessed the good confession in the sight of many witnesses.

2 Timothy 1:7 For God didn't give us a spirit of fear, but of power, love, and self-control.

2 Timothy 4:18 And the Lord will deliver me from every evil work, and will preserve me for his heavenly Kingdom. To him be the glory forever and ever. Amen.

Hebrews 4:12 For the word of God is living and active, and sharper than any two-edged sword, piercing even to the dividing of soul and spirit, of both joints and marrow, and is able to discern the thoughts and intentions of the heart.

Hebrews 11:32-34 What more shall I say? For the time would fail me if I told of Gideon, Barak, Samson, Jephthah, David, Samuel, and the prophets, who through faith subdued kingdoms, worked out righteousness, obtained promises, stopped the mouths of lions, quenched the power of fire, escaped the edge of the sword, from weakness were made strong, grew mighty in war, and caused foreign armies to flee.

Hebrews 12:9 Furthermore, we had the fathers of our flesh to chasten us, and we paid them respect. Shall we not much rather be in subjection to the Father of spirits, and live?

James 1:13 Let no man say when he is tempted, "I am tempted by God," for God can't be tempted by evil, and he himself tempts no one.

James 4:6-8 But he gives more grace. Therefore it says, "God resists the proud, but gives grace to the humble. Be subject therefore to God. Resist the devil, and he will flee from you. Draw near to God, and he will draw near to you. Cleanse your hands, you sinners. Purify your hearts, you double-minded."

James 5:16 Confess your offenses to one another, and pray for one another, that you may be healed.

The insistent prayer of a righteous person is powerfully effective.

1 Peter 5:6-7 Humble yourselves therefore under the mighty hand of God, that he may exalt you in due time, casting all your worries on him, because he cares for you.

1 Peter 5:8 Be sober and self-controlled. Be watchful. Your adversary, the devil, walks around like a roaring lion, seeking whom he may devour.

1 John 2:27 As for you, the anointing which you received from him remains in you, and you don't need for anyone to teach you. But as his anointing teaches you concerning all things, and is true, and is no lie, and even as it taught you, you will remain in him.

1 John 3:8 He who sins is of the devil, for the devil has been sinning from the beginning. To this end the Son of God was revealed: that he might destroy the works of the devil.

1 John 4:4 You are of God, little children, and have overcome them; because greater is he who is in you than he who is in the world.

2 John 1:7 For many deceivers have gone out into the world, those who don't confess that Jesus Christ came in the flesh. This is the deceiver and the Antichrist.

Revelation 12:9 The great dragon was thrown down, the old serpent, he who is called the devil and Satan, the deceiver of the whole world. He was thrown down to the earth, and his angels were thrown down with him.

Revelation 12:10 I heard a loud voice in heaven, saying, "Now the salvation, the power, and the Kingdom of our God, and the authority of his Christ has come; for the accuser of our brothers has been thrown down, who accuses them before our God day and night."

Revelation 12:11 They overcame him because of the Lamb's blood, and because of the word of their testimony. They didn't love their life, even to death.

Revelation 19:7 "Let's rejoice and be exceedingly glad, and let's give the glory to him. For the wedding of the Lamb has come, and his wife has made herself ready."

Common Demonic Spirits, Idols, and Manifestations

abandonment abortion abuse accusation addiction adultery affliction agitation alcohol ambush angel-worship anger anguish Antichrist anxiety apathy apprehension arguing arrogance ashamed astrology Ayurvedic-medicine backbiting Bahaism belittling betrayal bickering bigotry bioenergetics bitterness black-magic blasphemy blood-oaths boasting body-work breakdown brokenness bruising brutality Buddhism burden caffeine cancer callousness cautiousness celebrity-worship channeling charms chi Christian-Science co-dependency comparison competition compromise compulsion compulsive-eating conceited condemnation confrontation Confucianism confusion conjuration contentiousness control corpse covetousness cowardice cravings criticism cruelty crushing crystal-ball cults curses danger darkness daydreaming deafness death debate deceit deception deductions defeatism Deja-Vu dejection demonic denial depression despair despondency destruction devouring disappointment disaster discontent discouragement disease disgrace disgust disobedience disorganization disrespect distress distrust divination divorce doom double-mindedness doubt downcast dread dream-catchers drivenness drugs dumb Easter-bunny ego elves embarrassment enemies Eniagrams entertainment envy error escapism ESP exhaustion exposure extravagance failure faint-hearted fall falsehood false-burden familiar-spirits fantasy fatigue fault-finding fear fearfulness feminism fetishes fighting flattery flaws fleeting foes foolishness forgetfulness forlorn formalism fornication forsaken fortune-telling foul frail fraternities Free-Masons frigidity frowning frustration fury gender-confusion genies gloating gloominess gluttony gossip greed guided-imagery guilt gurus hardness harlotry harm harshness hatred headache heartache heartbreak heartless heaviness heavy-hearted heckling hex hiddenness Hinduism hip-hop hoarding homeopathy homicide homosexuality hopelessness horoscope horrified hostility humanism humiliation hurt hyperactivity hypnotism hypocrisy hysteria idleness idolatry immorality impatience importance impurity inadequacy incantation incense incest incoherence inconsistency indecision indifference ineptness inferiority infirmity ingratitude iniquity innuendo insanity insecurity insomnia intellectualism intolerance iridology Islam isolation jealousy Jehovah's-Witness Jezebel judging killing kleptomania laziness legalism leprechauns lesbianism lethargy Leviathan levitation lies limitations listlessness lodges loneliness lust lying madness malicious mania manipulation martial-arts masturbation meekness Mensa metaphysics mind-binding misery mockery morbidity Mormonism Mother-Earth murder necromancy nervousness New-Age obsession occult oppression orphan Ouija-board overwhelm pain palmistry paranoia passivity pendulum perfection perishing persecution perverseness pharmakeia phobias pilates pit plague plot poltergeists poverty pouting powers-and-principalities prejudice pressure presumption pretension pride procrastination profanity prostitution psychology punishment quarreling racism rage railing rape rationalization rebelliousness Reflexology Reiki rejection religiosity resentment resistance restlessness retaliation retreat ritualism rock-n-roll Rolfing rotting roving rudeness Sadism sadness scapegoat scatter schemes schizophrenia Scientology séance secrets seduction selfishness self-centeredness self-delusion self-pity self-reward self-righteousness senility shame Shintoism shyness skepticism slander slaughter sleepiness slippery slothfulness snare sophistication sorcery sororities spells spiritism spirit-guides spitefulness stealing stinginess stoicism strife strong-arm stubbornness stumbling stupor subdue suicide superiority superstition suspicion Taoism tardiness tarot-cards tension terror theatrics Theosophy Therapeutic-Touch threats timidity tiredness tolerance Tooth-Fairy torment Transcendental-meditation traps treachery troubles unawareness unbelief unclean unconcern underachievement unfairness unfaithfulness ungratefulness ungodly-grief ungodly-sorrow unreliable unresponsive unworthiness vanity vex victimization vile violence violent Voodoo war wastefulness water-witching weariness white-magic whoredom wickedness wiles willfulness witchcraft withdrawal worry wounding wrath wrong

*This list includes objects of occultism, but is not a complete list of demonic spirits, idols, or manifestations.

Common Godly Spirits and Manifestations

abundance acceptance adoption alertness alive
attentiveness availability belief blessing burning caring
character clarity compassion completeness contentment
counsel courage creativity delight deliverance dependability
desire determination diligence discernment discipline
discretion endurance enthusiasm excellence faith
faithfulness fear-of-God fervency forbearance forgiving
freedom freewill fruit generosity gentleness glory
goodness grace gratefulness gratitude guard happiness
healing helpfulness Holiness honesty hope hospitality
humility integrity joyful joyous justice kindness knowledge
life Light limitless living long-suffering love lowly loyalty
mercy might miracle morality obedience orderly pardon
patience perseverance power praise preserve prevail
promise Prophecy prosperity protecting punctual pure purity
quiet radiant redemption reliability rescue resourceful
respect responsible responsive rest restoration reverence
Righteousness safety salvation security self-control serving
sincerity Spirit steadfastness stewardship strength
supplication thankfulness thankfulness triumph trustworthy Truth
understanding unfailing unity unshakable victory virtue
vision willingness wisdom wholeness worthiness

Can You Help?

I appreciate feedback, and I love hearing what readers have to say. Your input helps to make subsequent versions of this book and future books better. Please leave an honest book review letting me know what you thought of the book. Share your favorite quote or share a photo or video.

There's a whole community praying for God's healing hand to touch every reader, and we'd love to praise the Lord with you to celebrate your victory! If you have a testimony of healing to share, please email FirebrandUnited@gmail.com.

Thanks so much!

Sallie Dawkins

Also By This Author

The Awakening Christian Series

The three-part, best-selling **Awakening Christian Series** shares Sallie Dawkins' testimony of discovering identity, potential, and purpose in Christ. A heart encounter with God in 2015 challenged Sallie's entire belief system. It was the beginning of the end of two-and-a-half decades of wavering faith and started her on a supernatural journey of discovery that rapidly transformed her life. Now an ordained

Christian healing evangelist, Sallie teaches through testimony, inviting born-again Christians to confront assumptions, doubts, and lies.

The Awakening Christian Series is a valuable tool for guiding believers into a more meaningful relationship with God and answers questions Christians can't, don't, or won't ask in church. If we don't know or believe that God is who He says He is, how will we ever know or receive the fullness of His love for us? And if we cannot love ourselves and who we are in Christ, how will we love others as they deserve to be loved?

The lessons Sallie shares about her journey of spiritual growth can benefit every born-again Christian. This series is suitable for individuals and small groups. Readers will find valuable resources and application questions at the end of each chapter. Sallie Dawkins will show you how God brought healing to her own life, and how He can do it for you, too!

Additional Resources

For Christians Seeking God's Promises for Healing, Identity, Purpose, Provision, and Wealth

Thoughtfully compiled by Christian Healing Evangelist Sallie Dawkins, these books of scriptures are helpful for supplemental or stand-alone studies of God's Word. All scriptures are from World English Bible (public domain).

God's Promises for Abundance of Healing is an indispensable resource for Christians eager to explore God's word on healing. Sallie experienced significant healing in her own life as she learned to seek God for revelation on this topic. She believes what God did for her; He'll do for you.

In Proverbs 12:18, we read, "The tongue of the wise heals" (WEB). God loves when we pray His words back to Him, but many Christians are unaware of how much God has to say about healing. Whether you're seeking self-healing or healing for others, God's word is good medicine!

You'll find over 800 scriptures referenced in this book. The index includes over 70 different categories to assist you in quickly locating relevant scriptures specific to healing spirit, soul, and body.

What we believe about ourselves affects what we think we can achieve. All of life begins with God and flows from our relationship with Him as our Savior and LORD. **Complete in Christ: Discovering Identity, Provision, and Purpose within God's Word** is an essential resource for Christians seeking to grow in their relationship with God.

God created us in His image, yet many Christians struggle to know Him more intimately. If we're to grow into the fullness of spiritual maturity, we must first accept that God is who He says He is. Only then can we comprehend our identity in Christ and believe that we are who He says we are.

This book includes over 1,000 scriptures indexed in over 130 categories, including Beloved, Blessed, Child, Chosen, Covenant, Deliverer, Favor, Gifts, Glory, Inheritance, Loving, Name, Power, Promise, Servant, Trust, and more!

Do you long to prosper in fiscal health for your home and business? God's healing power is not only for your body; it's also for your finances!

Aligning our thoughts, words, and actions with God's Word is the beginning of wisdom for growing in spiritual maturity. **God's Wisdom for Wealth: Flourishing in Family and Business** is a compilation of scriptures created especially for Christians desiring wisdom for leadership and wealth in work, business, and family.

These scriptures teach us how to be exemplary employees, employers, servant-leaders, Kingdom Ambassadors, sons, and members of the Body of Christ. Christian healing evangelist Sallie Dawkins has thoughtfully compiled over 800 scriptures indexed in over 100 categories related to Prosperity, Provision, Stewardship of resources, Rest, Wisdom, and Wealth. When we prosper, we honor the KING of Kings!